a
PARIS
notebook

For John & Blanka —
Best wishes!

Charles

3/26/09

a PARIS notebook

by

C. W. GUSEWELLE

THE LOWELL PRESS / KANSAS CITY
1985

Cover design by Dorothy Day
Back cover photograph by Bob Barrett

First Edition
Second Printing
Copyright © 1985 by C. W. Gusewelle

Library of Congress Cataloging-in-Publication Data
Gusewelle, C. W. (Charles W.)
A Paris notebook.

1. Gusewelle, C. W. (Charles W.)—Journeys—France—
Paris.   2. Authors, American—20th century—Biography.
3. Paris (France)—Description—1975-   .   I. Title.
PS3557.U833Z47   1985   818'.5403 [B]   85-18219
ISBN 0-932845-01-0

This book was photocomposed in Janson type and
printed on acid-free paper
in the United States of America by
The Lowell Press, Kansas City, Missouri.

ACKNOWLEDGMENT

These Paris essays appeared first in
The Kansas City Star. I am grateful
to Michael E. Waller, *The Star's*
editor and my friend, for imagining
that they belonged.

To Katie, to Anne,
to Jennie

BEGINNINGS . . .

A plane delayed in leaving meant that at the other end, the next midday, the Paris train was missed. The station board showed another train three hours later, so it was an inconvenience, nothing more. Briefly it occurred to me to telephone ahead to advise the hotel of the slight change in schedule. But our reservations had been confirmed long in advance, and anyone knows that traveling is an uncertain business. Surely it wasn't worth the bother of a call.

So we left our stack of cargo—the gear for seven months in France—in a porter's charge, and set off, my two teenage daughters and I, to poke around the capital of Luxembourg duchy. We saw a bit of the city. The three hours passed. Our detritus was heaved aboard. The train ran south into France, then westward down the long green fold of the Marne valley to Paris. And two taxicabs delivered us from the Gare de l'Est across the Seine at evening to debark a final time on the sidewalk outside the Hôtel de France in the Rue Monge.

The girls sat atop the baggage mound outside, while I stepped into the hotel's tiny lobby and passed the Telexed confirmation across the reception desk to a small, dark-skinned man who looked at it, then back at me, with the saddest eyes you can imagine.

"Yes," he murmured. "But you were to come at 6 o'clock"— he looked at the clock, which said after 9. "And now your rooms are taken." His own regret was plain. "Until 8 o'clock I kept your places. But then, when I did not hear, I had to give them. I am only the night clerk, and those are my instructions. So the hotel is *complet*. There are three big expositions now, and I am afraid all Paris is *complet*."

My whole life did not pass before my eyes. But the possible

shape of that night revealed itself—a night huddled somewhere on benches or curbs. *Idiot,* screamed an inner voice, not at the man behind the desk but at the fool who stood before him in my body. *For lack of a telephone call. Idiot!*

I went out to the sidewalk to report.

"There's a problem about our rooms," I said. People passing to and from their revels scarcely turned to look. Castaways are common on the streets of Paris, though usually not so elaborately burdened.

"Then we'll have to go to another hotel," one of the girls said logically. Fathers are counted on to be capable and provident. Fathers do not oblige their children to sleep atop duffel bags in the miasmic open air of alien cities. If small problems do present themselves, fathers solve them with dispatch.

One of the current expositions was a European jazz festival. Street bands were playing on nearly every corner of the quarter, the gaiety mocking my predicament. Blue night was gathering. I went back inside.

"Look," I said to the clerk, "could you try some other places?"

"I will try," he said. "But I am afraid—"

The Hôtel de France is one of that prolific class of small Left Bank hotels offering spotless comfort at a bearable price. He telephoned all the others in that same category. And several in the luxury class. And some others, far away in different quarters, that may have been wretched holes. How many he called I couldn't say, dizzy as I was with fatigue and despair. But two dozen anyway, maybe more. The conversations with his colleagues on those night desks were urgent, courteous, brief. And then, looking up finally with eyes even sadder than before, he sighed and closed the directory.

"Complet," he said. "In all Paris tonight there is not a room."

One daughter came in from the sidewalk, which was emptying of people. About the providence of fathers they were beginning to have doubts. It was after 11 o'clock now, and 34 hours since the last bed.

"Let me ask you," I said to the small, dark man. "In my place, what would *you* do?"

"Possibly there is some friend you could go to?"

"No one. I have the names of people who may be friends later. But none yet."

What seemed like several minutes passed in silence. And then he picked up the phone.

"So," he said. "I will call my friend, and he will take you to my room. It is far from here, and it is a small room. I live alone, and my clutter is there. But there is a bed. A bed, a table—it's what I have. And tomorrow, if someone leaves the hotel, you may come back here."

That was the choice: this stranger's room, or the street. I tried to thank him.

"I do it for your daughters," he said. Not for the fool, for the fool's daughters. But offered so shyly, with such humility, that I don't expect ever to receive a more elegant gift. Our bags we left at the hotel, taking only things for the night. The friend came and guided us there, and laid out bed linens new from the packages, never used. And finally, sometime after midnight, we slept—the girls pressed close together on the single narrow bed, me crossways at the bottom, their feet across my back, my own feet resting on a wooden chair, one blanket covering us all.

And when, a minute later, the dawn came over the chimney pots and into the single window, I got up quietly and crept out and down to the street for the finest pastries I could find. And brought those back and we ate them and took stock of where we were.

He had said the apartment was small. Four steps exactly, it measured, from wall to wall. Besides the bed, a table and four chairs and a primitive cabinet of unpainted wood completed the furnishings. Atop the cabinet was a small transistor radio, a corkscrew, a hookah pipe for his occasional smoke; and on the floor, an electric space heater and a pressing iron. Offset from the room was a sink, a counter and, separated from that by a plastic curtain, a stool and shower—all this measuring one step by a bit more than two. In the sink were pink glass dishes stacked to be washed. On a hotplate beside it, a pan with the remains of something cooked. Wedged behind the exposed water pipes against the wall were his toothbrush, razor and hairbrush.

And that is all: the few needs and slender comforts of a man alone, living frugally, swallowed up in the immensity of a city far from his home, which, as we would learn, was a place you might not even be able to point to on a map—the island of Mauritius, a dot of habitation far out in the vastness of the southern Indian Ocean.

Oh, yes. There was one other article in the room, which I would not have mentioned but which my daughters spoke of later when, coming from his all-night duty at the hotel, he insisted on taking us for coffee in a café and refused to let me pay.

"We like your bear," one of them said, with the wonderful artlessness of the young.

On his bed, when we had come there in the night, was a large Teddy bear, woolly haired, worn from the years of being held by a boy and then a man.

"Yes," said Soyam—for by then we knew his name. "I am by myself, and the bear is my friend. He is Guillaume."

All that has been weeks ago. It seems even longer. We are established now in our apartment in a pleasant quarter—lodgings that, to Soyam, when he comes to supper here, must seem spacious almost to excess, although his goodness doesn't let him speak of that or even, possibly, notice.

We only give what we have, as he did—though he gave much more.

Beginnings

Years from now, when their recollection of all the rest has paled, I know that my daughters will remember their first night in Paris, their first night ever abroad. Not for anything it told them about this city or the French, but for what they learned about the surprising, the saving, decency that is still possible in the world.

—Paris, June 1984

Summertide

1

IT IS NOT TRUE, as some would have you believe, that apartments in Paris are both impossible to find and savagely expensive. Not both. But always they are one or the other.

If funds are limitless, a place to live may easily be had by looking in the classified advertisements of any morning paper— *Le Figaro* or the Paris edition of the *Herald Tribune*—or one of the several weekly publications in which lodgings are offered for sale or rent.

Here, for example, on a page open before me, is listed a furnished studio near the Avenue Montaigne, in a fashionable quarter not far off the Champs-Élysées. Beautiful old building, the ad says. Fifth floor, no elevator. One small bedroom, petite kitchen, bathroom. Fifty-five habitable square meters—a bit more than six steps by 10 steps in all. References are demanded. A three-month deposit must be put up in advance. The rent: more than $1,400 monthly at the current favorable rate of exchange. Utilities not included.

If that is what you have in mind, finding an apartment in Paris is the easiest thing imaginable, the work of a day or two at most. But if such a place happens not to suit your purse or your needs—if it's a family you have to accommodate and you have not recently come into the directorship of a Fortune 500 company—then you have before you an ordeal of some importance.

Soon after dawn you fly out to the news kiosk and collect the papers to bring back and read over breakfast in the hotel. Each morning's listings deliver new blows to your solar plexus. Days can pass into weeks that way. Your hotel bill grows longer. The hotel-keeper's smile becomes thin, his manner strained. He is watching to see if you are trying to slip your baggage out. Presently it occurs to you that, although Paris is a lovely city, Peoria or Kalamazoo might have been a more sensible place to live and work.

In spite of all this, *we are installed.*

By incredible exertions and even greater luck, by prayers and wheedling and the expenditure of—for us—a dizzying sum of francs, we have a home. For the first five days we will have no gas or electricity, no means of cooking or lighting the place, nor any telephone by which to make contact with the wider world. But the situation on apartments being what it is, one daren't quibble over incidentals.

There is much paperwork in such a transaction—contracts to be signed in duplicate, dealings with the bank, assurances of solvency to be produced, receipts to be executed and initialed. All this is done with grave formality in an agent's office.

The owner is one Monsieur Demeulenaere. His sister, a stylish, high-strung and somewhat breathless woman, came with me to make an inventory of the contents. Her brother, she said, had been transferred temporarily to his firm's branch in Cairo, Egypt, and she was handling his affairs in his absence. Hastily she led me through the flat. Two smallish bedrooms it has, for the four of us. Also a sitting room, with an alcove to the side of that for eating; a small entry hall; a kitchen more or less equipped; a *salle de bain* with lavatory, bidet and tub, and two—yes, count them, two—of what the French refer to discreetly as water closets.

I accepted the inventory without amendment, since it was handwritten in French and could not be read in any case. The sister gave me two sets of keys, collected up her copies of all the papers and fled out, plainly glad to be shut of her responsibility.

And so we became the formal occupants of the place.

Our motley of belongings—amounting to 14 valises, duffels and random lesser containers—we transported across the city by taxicab. Two taxicabs, actually, in stately caravan, from the little Hôtel de France in the Rue Monge. The hotel's proprietor came out to wave goodby at the curb, his wife as well, both much relieved, all smiles again now that our account had been settled.

About Monsieur Demeulenaere, whose bed I'm sleeping in, I know practically nothing—about what his business is, or how it happened to take him to Egypt. But I hope earnestly he prospers at it. And that it keeps him there a while.

2

OUR WINDOW, which is very tall and wide, opens to the northwest, looking across the thick-foliaged crowns of a row of chestnut trees to the faces and small *balcons* of higher buildings, and over the slate and metal roofs and tile chimney pots of smaller ones.

In the home we have lately come from, people just now are going to their beds. But here the buildings across the trees are in full sunlight, although the street five floors below still is in shade. And on a ledge over our window a pigeon chortles to announce the morning.

The air at this hour, in fact at every hour, is surprisingly cool. It is like the air of the American far north, or of the mountains—warm in sun, sharp-edged in shadow. The summer, we have been told, has come late and strangely to Paris this year. I only know that with our window open we wake happily under two blankets in the morning. Two blankets in July! And the square of sky the window shows us might, in its hue and depth and clarity, be an early autumn sky.

We live in an elbow of the river.

From its rising not far from Dijon in the hills of Burgundy, the Seine winds its way northwest, gathering size and majesty, to enter Paris at the lower eastern corner and cut an arc through the city. Under the famous bridges it glides, strong and dark—past Notre-Dame and the Gothic piles of administrative and judicial buildings. Rejoining after the second of two islands, the river continues on beside the Louvre Palace, the Tuileries Garden, the Place de la Concorde and the Grand Palace at the top of the curve. Between the Eiffel Tower on the left, or south, bank and the Palace of Chaillot on the right, the Seine bends southwest to complete its arc—but soon loops sharply back to north again, to resume its coiling journey toward Le Havre and the English Channel.

And it is here, in that crook of the river, to fix the place exactly, that we will make our lives a while.

Walk just a short distance along the cool-shaded street below and you will come to a bridge, the Pont de Saint-Cloud, crossing to the suburb of that name which is visible only as a forested prominence to the west. Nearer, if one leans a little from the window and looks to the right, there is a handsome, slender-steepled church whose name, like most else about our immediate surroundings, we do not know.

Nearer still, at the end of this block, on a corner where a narrow street empties into a circle with a garden at its center, can be seen the purple awning of the café La Rotonde. It is not the same Rotonde made notorious a generation ago by artists and poseurs sitting at its tables. This one is a place of the neighborhood, still waiting for fame.

Nearest of all, at the very entrance of the apartment, is a tidy triangle of greenery—hedge, a scrap of grass, roses in scarlet bloom. And that is most of what we know or can see from our window.

The concierge of our building is Madame Freguin. Her husband, I believe, is Jean-Pierre, though I am bad about names. They are in their late 20s or possibly their early 30s. Madame Freguin is short, with black hair, sparkling eyes, a slight inclination toward roundness and a disposition so sweet, so cordial, that I think she must have been by origin a country girl. Always she is smiling—a happy and yet somehow secret smile that intensifies, both in happiness and secrecy, when her husband is nearby.

The husband—Jean-Pierre, or whatever his name in fact is—is clever with his hands. Yesterday he came and fixed, in a minute, the plumbing that had become corroded and nonfunctional during this apartment's long disuse. Electricity and telephone one can do without for a time. But the toilette, he declared, is *indispensable*.

That was his word for it, and I unreservedly agreed.

The telephone we will have in another day, the electricity for light and gas for cooking in two more. Meantime, we make cold camp, feasting on things bought fresh from shops on the next street behind, taking walks through the long evenings that are full light until after 10. Then coming back to read a little from a book together by candlelight before bed.

The book is one a friend gave me before leaving. In part, at least, it is a story about books themselves, and one of the characters in it, a small boy, is overtaken by wonder at how many things they can contain. Adventure, passion, wars and storms—all are there, forever taking place unnoticed between the closed covers, without an audience until some reader happens to open the pages and enter in.

I was struck, reading beside the candle last night, that that is exactly how these coming weeks and months lie before us, with all the adventures unsuspected, all the friends still unmet, the lives unknown. All of it there between covers that it is up to us to find ways to open.

3

Live in another man's home and you are always, in some measure, a prisoner of his taste.

What I know of Monsieur Demeulenaere I know only by what he has left behind of his belongings. But this slender information does not excite in me any great wish to know him better.

On the walls of the sitting room—or, as he might prefer to have it called, his *salon*—hang three prints, two Gauguins and one Cézanne, small and of fairly poor quality, and two others by some deservedly less-well-known artist. Also a larger original oil painting of the standard sylvan scene—a castle, gauzy trees, shepherds and such—in that hasty, commercial technique by which artists make their uncertain living from stalls along the river's left bank, fronting the Île de la Cité. And, finally, a hammered copper plate.

In one corner stands an oval table whose base is painted to resemble a ship's compass of antique style. Mounted in the table—part of it, actually—is an enormous globe, representing the world as it would have looked on ancient maps. The globe, colored brown to give the impression of age, does not turn easily on its pivot. It can hardly be made to turn at all, in fact. But never mind. My suspicion is that Monsieur Demeulenaere is satisfied simply to have it there, like the prints on the walls and the copper plate from somewhere, to announce his awareness of the arts and of the world.

In the corner opposite the globe is a writing desk and it, too, is chiefly decorative. As with nearly all desks of that kind, its front when folded out is much too flimsy for any kind of serious writing. A leather couch and two chairs complete the room.

The dining alcove, where I am working now, is dominated by a piece of furniture called, I believe, a *bibliothèque*—a combination cupboard, dry bar, bookshelves and glass-fronted cabinet in which are displayed a pewter dish and bowl, a candy server, two brass candlesticks, a ceramic pitcher, ashtrays, boxes with matches in them and other oddments.

In the whole of this *bibliothèque,* which translates to mean library, there is but one shelf of books, the other shelves all being taken up with bric-a-brac. The books are a matched set—Dostoevski, Zola, Flaubert, Stendhal, Dumas and other classics. Bound to look like leather, gilt-embossed, they are the kind made and bought to ornament a room. None has ever been opened, although as our French improves it is conceivable we may violate some of them.

Besides this table and six chairs, there are a *ficus* Benjamin and several other potted plants allowed to wilt and drop their leaves from neglect. What else to tell? Bedrooms are bedrooms, a kitchen is a kitchen, a bathtub a bathtub and a *toilette,* God knows, a toilet.

I have gone through all the nooks of the writing desk and every other drawer to see if he might have left something else that would give a clearer idea of his nature. There was a plumber's advertising card, a form letter from an insurance company and the instruction manual for a telephone attachment he bought but evidently never installed or learned to use.

Apart from these, nothing.

So I am left with this incomplete (and perhaps unfair) picture of the man: smug in his attainments, pleased with his possessions, with a certain vain sense of himself but no time for, or much real interest in, matters of the mind. But then there is the cat, for which I am almost willing to forgive him anything.

I don't know if it is an expensive piece or common. For all I care it might be cast of heavy plastic. Ten inches long and seven high to the points of its pricked ears, it reclines beside a lamp at the parlor window, peering out through the leaves of the wilted plants. Deep brown, the cat is, almost black, with two amber beads for eyes. And at a certain hour of evening, when the late sun slanting through the window strikes those amber eyes alive, the presence of the little statue fills the room, reminding us of our own cats that we have left to someone else's care.

It does not seem like an object that Monsieur Demeulenaere would have chosen for himself, for among his other things its vitality seems strangely out of place.

I think he must have received it as a gift.

4

IMAGINE THAT YOU are a pebble dropped in a still pond. From the immediate point of falling, circles spread—distinct at first, then fainter and slower as they pass farther out. That is how one's perimeter of known things widens in a strange place, among strange people. Except that the pond is not still. It churns with life.

So far our comfort zone, in which we have begun to feel at home, extends some two blocks. The street our window looks down upon is residential. The one behind is commercial—many fine old buildings of stone or brick, three to five stories high, with apartments and iron balconies and flowering window boxes on the upper floors, and shops below.

Beginning on the opposite side and making a brief circuit, you go from a bank's offices, on the corner, down past Bernadette's Coiffure, then a natural food store, a *parfumerie,* an optical shop, a coffee house and bar, a dealer in sausages and horseflesh, Yves Martin the florist, another hairdresser's, another bar, an ice cream parlor.

Crossing the Rue de Bellevue and continuing the second block, you find Le Méditerranée, a combination bar, restaurant and small hotel, where men of North African extraction sit at the sidewalk tables to read newspapers in Arabic, speak wistfully of warmer latitudes and watch for girls passing by. Beyond that is another tavern, the Bar des Cinémas, which appears to be permanently defunct; a tire store; a clothing shop, closed for summer redecoration, and something called the Salle de Jeux, which turns out—heaven help the French—to be an arcade of electronic games.

Toward the end of that block there is one of the numberless small branches of Felix Potin, a convenience chain; then a children's clothing store and, finally, another tobacco shop and bar, Le Narval, whose sidewalk tables attract a different crowd than Le Méditerranée's. That is more or less the boundary of the known, except that just beyond the cross street is a large establishment called Prisunic, a combination grocery and variety store where one can find nearly anything from girdles, bedsheets and disposable diapers to wine, fresh mushrooms and melons and berries of the season.

Fifteen minutes farther on by foot is the post office, which we have located, though it is far out in *terra incognita*. And a few steps down that second side street is La Fromentine, a *pâtisserie*—or pastry shop—operated by a man named Billou. Monsieur Billou himself I don't much care for. He affects short pants, sandals, silk shirts, medallions around his neck and a condescending air. I think he is practicing for his next life on the Riviera. Because, growing rich on the weakness of his fellow-man, he makes pastries you would kill for.

In our first days here, every walk seemed somehow to end at La Fromentine. Only by the most deliberate act of will can you make yourself pass on by without popping in for a quick 2,000 calories. Mercifully, Monsieur Billou drew down his shade yesterday and closed for a month, in accordance with the law regulating employees' vacations. Already we count the days. The Rue de Silly is the small street his shop is on—Silly Street.

Maybe you know that street. It's the one that leads to Fat City.

Returning quickly, then, you pass a butcher's stall for beef, mutton, tripe and birds; a stationer's and newsstand, Le Clap's bar, a little sporting store called Tennismania, a former movie theater taken over now by some proselytizing religious organization. And recrossing the Rue de Bellevue, you are back again at this building, which occupies most of one side of the block, with an automotive service station on the ground floor.

So, while our area of known turf may be small, it suffices. There are places for buying fruit and cheese, croissants, tobacco, newspapers, wine—the essentials—as well as for having one's hair cut or car repaired, if one has either hair or car. And just at the corner, directly facing the apartment, is the entrance to the métro, the Paris subway. At 29 cents a ride, that is our gateway to the still-mostly-uncharted reaches of the wider city.

5

UNLIKE THE NEW YORK subway, which arrives with a scream of grinding metal and a blur of spray-paint graffiti, driving a hot hurricane of stinking wind ahead of it along the tunnel, the Paris métro comes gliding civilly, silently, often on rubber wheels.

One moment there is nothing. Then a faint glow of reflected light can be seen at the bend of the wall, a little way up the dark tube from the lighted platform. Then, in an instant, the hurtling train appears, the operator sitting impassively with folded arms behind the glass of the first coach—the whole system evidently regulated by computers.

Briefly the train arrests itself, clean and inviting. Then, with a muted buzz of warning, the doors slide quietly shut again. And the machine—usually five coaches or six in tandem—speeds away toward Odéon, Invalides, Place de Clichy or some other of the nearly 300 stations on 15 lines that lie, like a fisherman's net, across the city.

The efficiency of the métro is a wonder. But its relative quietness is the most surprising. Imagine, then, how horrific it is to see someone down and disabled on the tracks, when no one on the platform knows exactly how many minutes—or possibly seconds—it will be before the swift and silent train will come.

I had not noticed the man. I was consulting the métro map on the station wall, or in some other way occupied. But I heard him fall—heard the collective gasp of the two dozen or so other waiting riders, and turned to see him down on the rails.

"Ooooh," the man said. The fall from the platform is four or four and one-half feet. He had struck and injured his leg against the track.

"Oooooh-ooooooh," he said again, with pain and sadness. He sat up and slowly, carefully, began drawing up his trouser leg to inspect the wound.

Now that they have put iron lattices around the upper platforms of the Eiffel Tower to discourage jumping, the métro has become a favored means of public suicide. As solutions to the problems of a life go, it is fast. It is above all certain. But the man down on the track was not one of those. He was just some poor devil of the alleys and benches, scabrous and filthy and wine-sodden to the outer reaches of senselessness. A man, in other words, who—except for luck—anyone might be. On his way to somewhere he had unexplainably fallen and hurt his leg. That was all he knew.

The things he had been carrying, wrapped in a newspaper, were scattered about him there in the deadly defile: some torn rags that might once have been clothes, a piece of a bread loaf whose crust was as dirty as his hands, a ball of twine, a broken umbrella. He could not get the pant leg up to see, so he sat rocking between the rails, holding his hurt. He turned his face, his eyes like burned-out coals, up toward the people who were looking down. "Oooooh," he told them, with fathomless regret.

A minute had passed, perhaps more.

At many métro stops, I have since learned, there is an alarm that may be sounded in such instances—one that must automatically halt the coming train. I don't know if there was one on that platform. In any event, no one thought to use it.

Would the man somehow regain his feet, then perhaps fall again—this time onto the charged rail? Or would the train come first? The platform was still as death itself. Some people turned away, so as not to have to see. Others were riveted with awful fascination. It occurred to me to run to the end of the platform and, when the train appeared in the tunnel, to wave my arms. It would have been useless; the machine could not have stopped in time. But it was the most I could imagine doing.

Then one man—just one, a lanky fellow in his 20s, in working clothes—did the unimaginable. He sprang down into the death zone, and seized the fallen *misérable* by his filthy clothes—the hurt one still saying "Oooooh" and even resisting a little. And shoved and dragged him back up to safety.

Then, when the train still did not come, he went back down to fetch the man's few belongings: the nasty piece of bread, the broken umbrella that would shelter him from nothing. Other hands carried the hurt man to a bench. People slapped the rescuer on his back. He seemed, himself, to be aghast and amazed at what he'd done—giddy-proud, and strutting a little, the way one is apt to after doing something brave but utterly unplanned.

The truth is that, in desperate moments, the ability to act is rare. A few have it. Most of us do not.

Then the train glided silently into the station, hesitated a moment, and—except for the one left moaning on a bench—carried us all away.

6

About the geography of their lives, the patterns of their days and the arrangements of their friendships, the young are fierce conservatives. Change disturbs them, seeming to endanger their not-yet-fully-formed sense of their own particular place in the cosmic order.

That is something one forgets in later years, when one has come to know that anywhere is home—and nowhere is.

So our daughters have been unsettled by the sudden translocation. Both of them have, but the younger one especially. Her moods are changeable as cloud shadows. One moment's excitement and fascination with the city can give way, in the next, to bleakest desolation. The episodes are brief, but they are profound.

She has taken to writing letters with a vengeance. I think she has written everyone she knows, some of them more than once. Nearly every day I am dispatched to the post office to bring home another dozen or so aérogrammes. There is something almost pitiful in this frenzy of correspondence. Soon, I think, the spasm will pass. Then, like those Americans at the sidewalk tables of the fancier cafés on the Place de l'Opéra, poring over the stock market quotations as they take their morning coffee, she will sit back to await the return on all her investments. And God help any friend or even remote acquaintance who does not immediately write back.

Before coming, I had this idyllic vision of how things would be for them.

Waking the first or second morning in our new place, they would go down to the street where, by luck or magic, a whole troupe of French children much like themselves—the same ages and interests—would immediately appear. At first, the French children would know a convenient bit of English. But that would be necessary only for a few days or a week at most. For despite any past deficiencies as language scholars, my daughters would open their mouths to speak and would find, with pride and astonishment, that their smattering of French words and phrases had overnight resolved itself into absolute fluency in the tongue.

Well, it isn't quite that way.

For one thing, the Paris district, including the suburbs, is a metropolis of some 8 million people, and it is almost wholly an apartment city. Sometimes you would think that all 8 million inhabitants must be adults, for children are rarely seen—not casually, at any rate, as they are along an American street. Children are in school, even far into summer. Coming home, they vanish quickly upstairs into the apartment, from which they seem to emerge again only infrequently, for picnics with their parents in one or another of the suburban woods or some other planned and fully self-contained excursion. So encounters are not easy.

For another thing, the subverbal grunts and stammers of the beginning French speaker are not transformed to eloquence by the mere accident of being in France. They still are grunts and stammers. The eyes of the natives glass over with anger and incomprehension.

Still, one reaches out for contacts as one must. The other afternoon, on the way to the bakery for the next morning's croissants, I left my older daughter, who is 15, at a table on the sidewalk outside Le Méditerranée, the café just down the block, thinking someone she would like to know might happen by. Coming back no more than a quarter-hour later, I found her flustered and unnerved, having in that short time attracted a seraglio of at least two dozen North African men in their 20s.

Another day, her younger sister, age 14, the one most smitten by loneliness, went trolling for friends in the area of the immense department store of central Paris, the Galeries

Lafayette. *Trolling* is a fisherman's term. It means to pass across the water, pulling your bait of choice slowly behind, to see what might be attracted. It is an indiscriminate kind of fishing, since you can never be certain of what you'll hook.

No American or French children of her age rose to the bait. Instead, she hooked another Arab, this one more than 30.

"Do you want a drink?" he asked her. Politely, she declined. But he followed after her. "Maybe you would like a drink," he suggested. Evidently it was his only English phrase. Again, a bit more firmly, she refused. "Ah," he said, as if struck by a new thought, "then what about a drink?"

Of all the many races and cultures that have flooded to this city, the men of the North African littoral seem, for reasons I can't explain, the ones worst afflicted by want of female companionship. The recommended response is rudeness—simply to look through them and past them, as if they did not exist.

In some way I sympathize with those men in their sad predicament. But I do not see, in their loneliness and my daughters', any prospect of a mutual remedy. Even so, the habit of rudeness is hard to learn.

7

IT IS REASONABLE, when after an interval of years you come back to a city like this one, to do the tourist things again. To visit the churches and take a boat ride along the river. To walk on a sunstruck morning down the Avenue Champs-Élysées from the Arc de Triomphe, at the top, toward the Tuileries at the bottom, with Paris spread on either side and beyond, and imagine you own the city. To get lost in the maze of the Louvre with several thousand other people, all trying to find the Mona

Lisa or the statue of Venus de Milo.

You do that almost with a sense of obligation, and mostly it is never as electric as it is supposed to be, or as you remember it once being. But this time there is no aftertaste of disappointment. There will be more chances. The season will turn. The summer crowds will leave and Paris will become a French city again, and we will stay. We will see her in all her weathers, in all her moods.

I have made only one nostalgic pilgrimage, to the little Hôtel de Nice at 155 Boulevard Montparnasse where I stayed my first time here as a young man 25 years ago. I paid then, if I remember right, nine francs for half a room that I shared with a friend. The hotel appears to have expanded—perhaps gotten more ground-floor space and enlarged the lobby, where before there was hardly more than a counter inside the door. And the rate now for a double room, with breakfast, is 250 francs a night.

Paris has prospered and, prospering, has changed. Modern buildings have gone up to alter—some would say disfigure—the skyline. Automobiles have multiplied and traffic is impossible. Prices have inflated. Once-ratty districts have become fashionable. And the collapse of empire in Africa and Southeast Asia has changed the human mix, for today's Parisian can as easily be ebony-skinned or saffron-skinned, or some shade between, as ethnic French.

My first impression was that the city had become somehow more stolid, more smugly conventional—that some of the magic of improvisation had gone out of her; that she had ceased to be a place of risk and extravagance and caprice, a place where things begin, and had become instead a city where, fat with success, things end.

And then one evening, just before dusk, we climbed the narrow streets of Montmartre to the church of Sacré-Coeur.

A crowd of several hundred had gathered—sitting, sprawling—on the wide steps leading up to the church, its white domes luminous in the declining sun. All in that assembly were young, and they had come there from half a hundred places in the world for no reason except to *be there* and to celebrate youth itself.

The air cooled. Guitars were gotten out. Voices rose up, singing some of the anthems of their generation—the Beatles' "Hey Jude" and Simon and Garfunkel's "The Sounds of Silence" and others. Bottles of red wine were passed from hand to hand. Montmartre, you hear, has gotten sleazy and a little rough, no place to be alone after dark. But who was alone? Sitting there on the stone steps, crowded close and touching, they were wrapped all together in the sweetest years of their lives.

The sun was gone, then. The modern buildings vanished in the blueness and only the old ones could be seen. Then the lights began winking on, until all of the city was spread like a firmament beneath today's children, where they sat singing and imagining on that hill. The voices came strong and clear. The wine slid innocently, harmlessly, down young throats.

And that's how it has always been. The city hasn't changed, grown portly. I have. Paris stays forever young, because each generation reinvents her in its time.

8

SHORTLY BEFORE NOON there was a knock at our door. Opening it, I found standing there an owlish little man, coat draped across his shoulders in the European manner. He introduced himself as Monsieur Farchakh, occupant of the apartment whose door is next to ours on the stair landing, and asked if I had heard any disturbance in the hall a bit earlier in the morning. I had not. With the big window open and my typewriter going, anything I hear is from the direction of the street.

He drew me into the hall to see his problem. His key would not fit in the door lock. Looking into the keyhole, it was clear the opening was blocked by some object, another key perhaps, inserted in the lock from the opposite side.

Monsieur Farchakh, who is Lebanese, explained that he was planning to leave tomorrow with his wife and daughter on a month's holiday to visit relatives in the old country—if going to Lebanon in these times for any reason can be called a holiday. Their packed valises all were inside the apartment. So was his money for the trip, which he had intended to take to the bank this very afternoon to change into Lebanese currency. The problem with the door could not have happened at a more inconvenient time.

A crowd began to gather on the landing. Madame Farchakh and the daughter appeared. Then the elderly woman whose door is the third one on our landing came out in robe and slippers. Yes, she said, she had heard a noise in the hall—at midmorning it had been, about 10 o'clock. She had peered from the peephole in her door but had seen nothing.

Madame Freguin, the concierge, came up on the elevator with her husband, Jean-Pierre, who was wearing a T-shirt and satin running shorts.

"You see it," Monsieur Farchakh told them, putting his key part way into the lock to demonstrate. "It will not go."

"He has been robbed," Jean-Pierre announced to the rest of us, although Monsieur Farchakh himself seemed not to realize it yet.

I rummaged through a kitchen drawer, found a long screwdriver and several other slender but unidentifiable instruments, and went back out and knelt in front of the lock. A hush descended as I poked around a while in the hole, having no idea at all what I was doing. "Impossible," the others said finally. But

I was glad that I had tried. I had shown myself to be, if ineffective, at least earnest.

"I will have to call a technician," Monsieur Farchakh said, and went to borrow the elderly neighbor's phone. Meantime, his nephew appeared, a strapping young man in his early 20s, and asked if he might look from our kitchen window a moment. Leaning perilously out, he could see from there that his uncle's window was ajar. Did I perhaps have a rope, he asked. I didn't. And anyway, I tried to tell him, it would be far too dangerous. He meant to affix the line to something in the kitchen and attempt a traverse of several feet across the sheer side of the building, without even a ledge, to another partly-open window five floors above the street.

"With a rope," he said, "it is not a problem." To a Lebanese, after what that country has suffered in the last decade, all dangers must be relative.

But before I had to participate in that, the locksmith arrived. After seeing him at work, "technician" was not a word I would have used to describe him. With a ballpeen hammer he beat the lock out of the door—just *beat* it out, fragments of wood and all—advising Monsieur Farchakh as he did this that it would cost more than 2,000 francs, nearly $250, to replace the mechanism.

"Les bijoux et l'argent," he muttered grimly between hammer blows. *"Toujours—les bijoux, l'argent."* Always the same, the money and the jewels.

The door gave way with a crash and the technician stood aside, pleased with his work. Monsieur Farchakh, the soul of hospitality, invited everyone in. His apartment filled up with the curious. The stereo had not been touched. Or the television. A cabinet door was open and some papers had been scattered on the floor, but otherwise there was no sign of ransacking. The family's packed suitcases were undisturbed. Then Madame Farchakh came out of the bedroom, her face desolate.

"Les bijoux," she said. Her jewelry was gone.

21

Her husband went into another room. The locksmith waited expectantly. Monsieur Farchakh called out the news.

"Et tout l'argent." All his money as well.

The locksmith nodded, then set about repairing the door he had destroyed. Monsieur Farchakh, pale and trembling, but still painfully courteous, apologized for having *déranged* us—that is, disturbed us. I didn't have the heart to ask if he would still be leaving tomorrow.

"We are all vulnerable," said the elderly lady who shares our floor. Shaking her head at the rising tide of wickedness in the world, she shuffled away in her slippers. And as soon as she closed her door, you could hear the dead-bolt turning.

9

IT WAS ONLY the briefest encounter. He got aboard the métro at Gobelins or the Place d'Italie, rode several stops, and then the doors of the car slid open and discharged him into the immensity of the city, never likely to be seen by us again. That was all. And yet so arresting he was—so astonishing a figure—that seeing him had been the principal event of the day. And that night, before bed, my daughters and I spent at least an hour talking about him, speculating.

Understand that summer has come finally to Paris. Not scorchingly, as it does to the American plain, but distinctly warm. Men go coatless to their work, and women wear their lightest, filmiest dresses. So, there on the métro was this man from somewhere in West Africa, Gabon or the Cameroons perhaps, judging from the blue-blackness of his skin. He was tall for someone from his part of the world, six feet and several inches. His solemn face gleamed like a mask of polished wood.

But it was his outfit that was remarkable.

He was perspiring furiously inside a suit of the heaviest woolen cloth you can imagine—that spiky, abrasive kind of wool that all boys remember from their first winter long pants. On his head was a black lambswool hat, like the Russian politburo is always photographed wearing as they stand in frosty weather atop Lenin's tomb to watch parades of their tanks and missiles. And on his feet he wore a pair of high-topped white tennis shoes.

Something may be lost in the telling, but take my word that he was quite a sight. And as he got to where he was going and stepped with grave dignity out of the car, the eyes of the other riders followed him with wonder and amusement.

What is the history of a man like that? That's the question that occupied us afterward, that night beside the open kitchen window, with the sounds of the city coming in from the street. My ideas about it may be cockeyed in small details, but I would bet that the general drift of them is close to the fact.

In past years, when the ruling hand of Europe reached round the world, France maintained an idealistic fiction. She insisted that her subject territories were not colonies at all, but overseas provinces of herself. And that their peoples were on the way, through long acculturation, toward being simply Frenchmen of a slightly different sort.

Then the "wind of change," as the British called it, blew empires suddenly away. But a notion as compelling as the one the French had planted dies hard—the idea of a quality of *Frenchness* transcending any accident of geography or race. All around the world, then, were left these diverse people, looking in some way to Paris as the center, not of their various nations but of their private and internal worlds.

Even after empire died they came here. And in greater numbers they still continue to come. Very different, some of those people are. So powerful a shaping force is this culture, of which language is a central part, that the immigrants are assimilated and do, in fact, fairly soon become nearly indistinguishable from the other French. But in the process, Paris and other major cities—and in lesser degree the country itself—also have been changed. And it is resentment of this change, however slight or however inevitable in history's light, that inspires the ugly racist slogans one sees from time to time on public walls.

Now, suppose that you were a man of some village in West Africa, trained up by the nuns in a French outpost school. And at some point you decided to try your life in Paris.

Europe you would have heard of as a far-off northern place, and cold. So you would prepare for that by getting a suit of the thickest, warmest fabric that money could buy. At some point in your country's independence struggle you would have been exposed to revolutionary literature. You might have seen pictures of those powerful Russian men in lambswool hats, and decided that someday you must have a hat like that. You would find that shoes made for the pointy feet of the French did not suit feet broadened by treading the forest path. Must a man go through his whole life, in the name of style, with his feet hurting? So you would discover tennis shoes, and put those on.

And thus you would finally come arrayed—the sum of your needs and of your borrowings, a man in whom the past and the future were uneasily met. Not understanding why people found you strange; why even your own children, in their time, would find you strange, being themselves almost wholly French.

That's how I tried to explain the man on the subway to my daughters.

A comic figure, certainly. But more than just that. A part of the longer, beautiful process of people's *becoming*.

10

Iт тАкеs nо expert judge of piano players to know determination when you hear it. And, whatever else, the occupant of the apartment directly above ours is devoted to the instrument.

Monday through Saturday mornings just after 8 o'clock, a bit later on Sundays, the music from up there begins. First, to loosen fingers stiff from sleep or the unseasonable chill of the morning, there is a full hour of keyboard exercises. Simple at first, they build in complexity and speed until the bursts of effortless notes, each crisp and distinct, tumble down like a melodic rain. Then there is a pause, while I imagine coffee being poured.

Finally, these preparations all complete, there commences a passage of what I believe is Chopin—an opening of majestic chords, *Daaah da-daa daaah.* Followed, after an exquisite hesitation, by two quick runs with the bass hand . . . *Thrrunk, thrrunk!*

To me it sounds wonderfully accomplished, but I am too easily satisfied. There is a scraping sound above as the piano bench is adjusted. The opening is heard again. And again. Each repetition sounding exactly like the one before, although evidently there must be some subtlety I am missing. Then, satisfied at last, the pianist moves on deeper into the piece. It goes like that until shortly after noon, when there is a break for lunch, since even an artist must take nourishment. The afternoon is much like the morning, but without the finger exercises.

On toward evening, there begin to be signs of fatigue, or possibly frustration. A wrong note will produce an irritable explosion of dissonance. Followed often by a frivolous detour into some popular song or even a few bars of jazz. But then discipline reasserts itself. The bench is readjusted with another scrape. The Chopin begins again.

Supper is a further interruption. Usually, afterward, the playing resumes. Evening is a time for exploration—for the preliminary sight-reading of some unpracticed but promising composition. Although always, to end the night's work, there will be one or two more renderings of the Chopin. Then the bench gives its last scrape on the floor above. And we all can sleep.

That's the unvarying agenda of the day—eight hours of practice at a minimum, except on Sunday, when there may be only six hours. Nothing else is ever heard from that apartment overhead. No sounds of talk or laughter, no television playing, no domestic noises from the kitchen or the other rooms. Only the music, the scrape of the bench and silences between.

The neighbors on our own landing we know by sight. But all the others in the building still are just faces on the elevator, without identities attached. So we can only speculate about which one of them this driven pianist might be. It isn't a child, we know, because the law requires even prodigies to sit in school. And not a man, because a single piece by Chopin, however brilliantly it is played, would not be sufficient repertoire to earn a living by. Surely it can't be anyone of great age—a regimen like that calls for the endurance of a mule.

So the possibilities narrow.

I have decided that our neighbor overhead must be a woman alone—a woman in her 30s or possibly her 40s. Once young and gifted, she was thought to have a future on the concert stage. But something went wrong. It may be she was pushed too hard too soon, and rebelled. Or was off her form at a critical recital. Whatever the reason, opportunity passed her by.

Now, with some small independent means, or supported by a gentleman patron who does not visit often, she passes the solitary days with her piano and her memories of better times. Her fingers still rush over the keys with miraculous dexterity.

Sometimes, as the music fills her modest room, she lets herself imagine that things are as they might have been. Beyond the footlights is a sea of indistinct faces. The hall is hushed. The conductor, his baton raised, turns to await her opening chord.

Daaah da-daa daaah . . . Thrrunk, thrrunk! Endlessly that scene is replayed.

It would not surprise me to know that it was the Chopin piece she was playing on the very day her fingers turned to wooden pegs and her chance was lost. Now she has a lifetime to get it absolutely right.

11

YESTERDAY'S CROISSANT is like an old girl friend, not much to look at and worse to spend time with. The bloom is both fragile and brief.

The schedule of our mornings, therefore, is governed by the time at which the day's fresh croissants can be gotten warm from the baker's oven. It may be that all Paris organizes itself around that moment, for hardly anyone goes to work before 9:30.

We have tried several of the neighborhood bakeries. But oddly enough the croissants we prefer come from the basement pastry shop of Prisunic, the food market and variety store a little way down our street. Each morning I wait on the sidewalk out front. And each morning the same scene is repeated. A crowd assembles—a dozen people or so, all with net bags or two-wheeled shopping carts.

The people look at their watches, which say half past the hour. Inside the three sets of locked glass doors, the floorwalker, a young man in a blue blazer with the store emblem on its pocket, looks at his watch, which does not agree with theirs. The store is ready for business. The new prices have been marked, the change counted, and the cashiers all are alert beside their registers on elevated stands, like tennis umpires. The clerk from lingerie comes coyly by and the floorwalker greets her warmly, with kisses on both cheeks—a bit *too* warmly, you might almost think. Then he returns to looking at his watch.

Grumbling begins to be heard among us there on the sidewalk. We watch the floorwalker through the glass doors and he watches us, all of us watching our watches. With an air of importance, then, he draws from his pocket the door key, attached to a chain. Each of the six doors in the three double sets must be unlocked individually. Slowly he does this. There is a premonitory shift forward by the people on the sidewalk. But stepping back, standing very erect, he raises his hand palm-outward to command a halt. It is his moment of maximum power. The doors are unlocked now. Only his will keeps us out.

Then, from deep inside the store, a buzzer sounds. The doors are pushed inward and the people rush through and on by, brushing the young man in the blazer aside on their way to the stairs leading down to the basement and the croissants, still warm to the touch, crusts flaky with brushed butter.

Every morning there is that ritual. And after the croissants have been gotten the day can begin. This morning I had just borne home the prize, gotten butter and jam from the refrigerator and laid the breakfast table when there was a rapping at our apartment door. Two young men stood there in suits, hair close-shorn, scrubbed-looking, smiling dynamically and shifting from foot to foot.

You know that look. You've seen it at your own door.

"Good morning," the tall one said in French, and thrust out his hand. It's always the tall one who speaks. The short one just stands and grins. "We have come to have a conversation," he said. "We are Witnesses."

"I'd have bet on it," I told him in English.

"*Comment?*" he said, which means Huh?

"What are we going to have a conversation about?" I asked him.

"We would like to tell you about the promises."

"Well, as a matter of fact, I'm not going to be here long."

"Who is?" he said happily. "That's why you should know the promises." I'd meant that I was only temporary in the neighborhood. But the idea of none of us being around very much longer appeared to give him great satisfaction.

"Can we come in?" he asked.

"My croissants will get cold."

"*Comment?*"

"I have six warm croissants. And if you come in and we have a conversation they'll get cold. So I think you'd better not."

Their smiles didn't even flicker.

"Well, thank you for being polite," the tall one said. "Some people are not even polite."

"Isn't this a Catholic country?" I said.

"No, not only that," he said. "It is, I think, a question of education."

"And timing," I told them as I closed the door. The Jehovah's Witnesses will make no headway in France by interfering with a man's morning croissants.

12

THEY CIRCULATE THROUGH the summer crowds of Paris like wolves in a pen of sheep. They can empty your pocket faster than any restaurant waiter and that, my friend, is *fast*.

I don't know how many Gypsies there are in the city—maybe

no one does. But hundreds, anyway. Possibly thousands. And now that few people ask to have scissors ground or knives sharpened, begging and petty thievery appear to be the main tribal vocations. They live outside the law. And the law, so meticulous in most other matters, does its best to ignore them.

Each morning the dark, sharp-faced women in head-scarves and outlandish flowered skirts take up station cross-legged on the sidewalks along the Champs-Élysées, spread a filthy rag on the pavement and display the latest and smallest of their spawn like sick kittens, while whining a reedy and tireless chant. Sometimes a coin is dropped on the rag. More often the river of people on the great avenue just parts and passes on. Then, at evening, the women and their children assemble in bands— teeth white in their sharp, brown faces as they laugh; the children suddenly quite healthy and nimble as fleas—and like a flock of gaudy birds all disappear noisily together down some métro stairway, away to wherever the secret place is that Gypsies spend their nights.

The children are not sent to school. In time, of course, they outgrow their usefulness for begging, but new ones are easily enough produced. Begging is only a sideline, anyway. Picking pockets is the serious work, whose mastery takes longer practice and more application than geometry or whatever else is taught at the lycée.

The French carry purses—both men and women do, though of different styles. In a crowd, they hold these purses flaps-in-ward against their bodies. They pay attention, and rarely are bothered. But any Parisian can circle on a map of the city three or four districts where, if you go there gawking and careless, you are all but certain to be relieved of some of your goods. Americans, with their inviting hip wallets and loose-flapping coats, eyes fixed raptly on shop windows or historic sights, leave a blood trail that a Gypsy can smell for blocks. A U.S. professor friend came through town last week with a group of students in tow. They left with a good deal less than they brought. Five of them had their pockets or handbags rifled in a single night.

One hears these stories and grows smug, imagining that one's own uncommon cleverness has kept the soft-handed wolves at bay. Arrogance makes you ripe.

It happened at the evening rush hour, in a crowded métro coach I had boarded at Rue Montmartre. The man beside me was needlessly stubborn, I thought, about making way for others to find standing room in the car. Stubborn or rude or both. I remember looking at him—swarthy, with the welt of a scar as wide as a wooden pencil down the near side of his face. An unpleasant looking rogue.

But his eyes were what registered most. Fixed not on me but somewhere to the side and behind, they glittered with a crazy yet absolutely focused intensity—the way I imagine a circus wire walker's eyes must look when he steps out on the cable 60 feet above the arena floor without a net. At exactly that moment, I think, his hand was in my pocket. The train came to the next stop. The car doors opened, and other riders crowded around us and out. The buzzer sounded. The doors began to close. In a sudden movement he was through them and gone, and I was riding on to the next station.

Even Gypsies don't get lucky every time. Being left-handed had saved me. He'd worked the pockets on the wrong side, missing money and passport, rejecting my glasses—with hands like his, who needs eyes?—and getting only a small notebook from which I'd taken all but the empty pages. So we celebrated, later, by going to a little Chinese restaurant several blocks down the street from our apartment and spending some of the money the thief didn't get.

To say that I hope he, too, was hungry that night, and that my notebook was what he ate for supper, does not mean that my mind is entirely closed to the argument that Gypsies are human beings with souls and civil rights and all that. Anger and

31

humiliation have to be tempered with admiration for anyone that good—at *anything*. And it would be interesting to know more about these ancient and devious people. Always in the autumn, I'm told, there is a big encampment of them in the Bois de Boulogne, the wooded park not far from where we live. I may even try to find some way to visit them there, being careful, of course, to carry or wear nothing I can't afford to lose.

13

A FRIEND DESCRIBED Parisians as gifted with a fine sense of occasion. One reason may be that their city provides so handsome a setting for spectacles, of which, this summer, there have been several in close succession.

First there was the huge demonstration over schools, provoked by a government plan—later withdrawn—to require private teachers to become certified in order for their institutions to continue to receive public subsidy. A modest enough proposal, that might have seemed. But constituents of the mostly-Catholic private schools saw it as the Socialist-foot-in-the-door of state control. So from all over France they came, carrying placards and banners and wearing buttons that said "Long Live Free Schools."

Whether there were nearly 2 million marchers, as the organizers claimed, or only 850,000 as the authorities reported, is immaterial. Either way there were a lot of people. Like human rivers they flowed through the sparkle of a sunstruck summer Sunday, singing and chanting in tune and even in time, converging in four mighty columns on the Place de la Bastille, the symbolic birthplace of republican France. Though the *gendarmerie* were positioned in force along side streets off the main routes of march, and though the next day's newspapers told of isolated incidents of unpleasantness, the mood of the day was predominantly festive—French people, outfitted as for a picnic, on a prodigious pedestrian outing over the cobbles and past the monuments of the city they love.

Three nights later, in the huge Roland Garros stadium a short walk from our apartment, the French team played for the soccer championship of Europe, having barely survived its semi-final match on a last-second goal that a *Le Figaro* headline writer said, with typical understatement, had "brought France back from hell." Only the Spaniards now stood between France and its first-ever championship. The streets emptied. Every television in Paris was tuned to the game. Bars and hotel lobbies filled up with people crowded around the tube.

The first half was scoreless. Then, in the 57th minute, the Spanish goalkeeper let a kick get through and the French team was on its way to victory. Minutes after the game's end, the city came alive again with processions of honking cars, boys throwing firecrackers and gentlemen staggering in various states of advanced disability. Long into the night the party went—at least until after we slept.

On July 14, Bastille Day, crowds were out early to line the Champs-Élysées for a patriotic parade. Mirage jets swooped low over the Arc de Triomphe and on down the great avenue, smoke canisters trailing the red, white and blue of the Tricolor. Units of all the services marched, including the hard characters of the Foreign Legion in their beige and red. Followed by a vast panoply of tanks, mobile cannons, rocket launchers, blimpish amphibians, wheeled bridges and other queer-looking military machines. And finally a formation of fire trucks. President François Mitterand, standing fully exposed in the back of an open car, passed slowly along the street.

Thus, with stylish pomp, was the national day celebrated by a country with neither a modern habit of murdering its leaders,

33

July 14, Champs-Élysées

nor any modern luck at winning wars. That night, while we watched from a loft near the Place du Trocadéro, there was a fireworks display like none other you'll ever see. For most of an hour, explosions shook the window glass, shook the very stones of the building, unfolding enormous fire-flowers over the river and wreathing the Eiffel Tower in a smoky glow.

In the most recent *fête,* Parisians—an estimated half-million of them—assembled again on the Champs-Élysées to watch men ride by on bicycles. It was the finish of the Tour de France, the three-week road race covering 2,500 miles, including punishing climbs in the Alps. The race ends with six laps up and down the avenue. The contest may take the cyclists' breath, but the view takes the spectators'.

In the office-apartment from whose balcony we had the luck to watch there were cold bottles of champagne and trays of confections laid out. Twelve times the riders flashed past below, among them a young Frenchman named Laurent Fignon, wearing the yellow shirt symbolic of his victory which had been assured days before in the mountains. The roar of the crowd sped with him along the street. Then, out of sight of most of the watchers, the race was over. Quicker than you would believe, the hundreds of thousands were absorbed back into the city.

This morning, on our errands out for provisions, it seemed that fully half the shops were padlocked and shuttered, the notes on their doors announcing a month's vacation closure. With the spectacles of summer concluded, Parisians have taken to the road.

14

THE TEMPERATURE RISES by a few degrees, the morning murk rolls eastward from the English Channel, the air thickens. And as the French abandon themselves to wanderlust, Paris sinks into its August sleep.

It is charmingly irresponsible. For those the exodus leaves behind, it is damned inconvenient.

One comes an alien, handicapped by language, to the enormity of this city and learns, by a series of small but hard-won triumphs, to make one's life work. One locates the premier pastry shop, and establishes connections at a bank to finance the excesses in éclairs and tarts. One learns which butcher does not weigh his thumb, and which kiosk has the newspapers one wants to read; learns whose apricots are plumpest and whose flowers the freshest; discovers where to get one's hair cut and where a duplicating machine is located. And also how to get to each of those places—the most direct métro line, the nearest stop.

Then, overnight, all that you have managed to learn becomes obsolete.

One morning you find the shade pulled down and a sign on the door announcing a month's vacation. Sometimes the note lists the address of another shop where you might do business. But, going there, you are unable to get the essential thing you need, and the proprietor cannot—or will not—say exactly where it might be found. I understand that every Paris summer is like this, with the abandonment beginning in July and worsening until, by August, the pulse of commerce beats very faint and slow.

The other day my typewriter broke and I went looking for a place to have it fixed. The first four repair shops bore holiday notices. The fifth turned out not to deal in machines at all, but stationery and such. The man there took an interest in the problem, though, and fixed the typewriter by poking inside it with a bent wire. A kind man, he was—refused any money for his help, and instead typed out on a scrap of paper a gracious salutation. But passing there the next morning I found his shades, too, were drawn. Like all the others, he had gone away to somewhere for a month. There is nothing to do now except treat the machine gently and pray that the part holds.

Shops along the main tourist avenues stay open, of course, since summer is their fattest season. So do banks and other such establishments, although their staffs may be halved by the annual flight from the city. Banking here, in the best of times, is an adventure. For a people so extravagant in many ways, the French have an odd fussiness about money. Maybe it is a nervousness born of not having known, from generation to generation, war to war, crisis to political crisis, what their currency might be worth. But for whatever reason, the banking laws are maddeningly complex.

It is easy to give your money to a bank, less easy to get it back. Remittances from abroad, unless directed to the specific branch where your account is held, may take as long as two weeks to be credited. Monies put in at one branch are not freely withdrawable at another of the same bank. If a deposit is made in dollars, it cannot be had in francs for as many as six days.

All of these transactions are conducted amid storms of paperwork, with much filling out of forms and affixing of seals. Bank officers run—not walk, *run*—breathlessly to and fro across the marble floors, fists full of documents. Yet nothing happens with dispatch. People waiting to do business fall asleep in their chairs or grow discouraged and wander back out to the street. And, at the end of it all, it develops that a certain officer, the only one able to consummate the matter at hand, is gone for her two-hour lunch break. Or, if it is August, is gone for a month to Saint-Tropez on the Côte d'Azur.

It has occurred to me, while struggling through this month, that Americans do not understand about leisure. How to work very hard, and with effect, we understand. Lunch does not last two hours. If the vacation season comes, somehow the shop is kept open, even if it means the proprietor himself must stay home. Prosperity rewards us—prosperity we are damned for in the world, but which we earn fairly, and at a price.

That is not to say one way is right, the other wrong. But from such choices flow consequences, against which it is pointless to rail.

15

ONE DAY FROM our window we noticed to the west, beyond the river, on the steep hillside between the first rooftops of the suburb of Saint-Cloud and the wooded ridge behind, what seemed to be a swatch of mown grass.

Living in a city of such size and density, one soon comes to hunger for a bit of space, for a scrap of untrammeled greenery. So that afternoon we crossed the bridge and climbed through the narrow streets of Saint-Cloud to investigate.

Even Parisians, accustomed to their apartment way of life, feel this yearning to be unenclosed. On pretty days they go to pass several hours in the Tuileries Garden or carry a picnic to the Bois de Boulogne, as we have done, beginning these excursions on métro coaches crowded with people all bound for the same destinations. The Bois is like any forested urban park, though its 2,200 acres may make it larger than some. There are people throwing Frisbees and boys kicking soccer balls and joggers panting past in sweaty platoons. There are places to eat, and lakes to paddle boats on, though all the boats already have been rented, and benches to sit on, though all the benches already are claimed. Also in the Bois there are two horse racing tracks and an amusement park, not places one would go in hope of finding space.

As for the Tuileries, which is so handsomely set—with the Place de la Concorde at one end, the Louvre at the other, the Seine running alongside—it is not a garden in any usual sense. Few flowers are to be seen. The tree-lined formal walkways, and even most of the areas under the trees themselves, are carpeted with a fine, gray chat. There are outdoor refreshment stands at whose tables one may sit an hour, hoping to be served. There are fountains where small children sail their boats, many children at once. The gravel walkways teem with people afoot, some with dogs on leashes, and with vendors of an assortment of souvenirs. What little grass one finds is covered entirely with oiled bodies revolving in the sun.

It isn't that these places are not handsome, even stately, in their way. The problem, as wherever people live compacted in such numbers, is only the sheer mathematics of demand.

So we climbed the crooked streets of Saint-Cloud that afternoon, not knowing what, if anything at all, the distantly-spied scrap of greenery might amount to. Turning a last bend, we came upon a formal garden with trees cut in topiary shapes, avenues of roses with blooms as large as dinner plates and, against a bank of grass, elaborately patterned beds of lower, blooming plants running on in intricate design around the far end of the ridge.

Looking back the way we'd come, we were rewarded with the most spectacular of views: the roofs of Saint-Cloud; the Seine, with barges plying down her and houseboats moored along her bank, and, beyond that, what seemed to be the whole of Paris at our feet. But that was only the beginning. A path led farther up and on, so we followed it. And entered into a place of serene beauty almost past the power of words to describe.

Other paths branched off that first one, a whole network of them, each leading to some different prospect of trees and flowering shrubs. At every turn, the woods opened ahead as in a painting, very dense and at the same time perfectly ordered— ancient oaks and great, dark pines and smaller trees of every imaginable kind, all arranged so that their shapes and the different textures and shades of their foliage combined in studied harmony.

It was as if armies of foresters and gardeners had had centuries and unlimited means to perfect their idea of a park. And then, finishing, had simply walked away.

The picture changed at each bend of the path. The dark grass between the trees and in the open glades was cut to a uniform height. Birdsong filled the lengthening afternoon. From a pond in one clearing wild ducks rose up and wheeled away among the trees. At intervals along the way there were benches. But except for one, where a woman sat alone and seemed lost in dreaming, they were all unoccupied. Two other walkers we saw at a distance, carrying a basket. And that was all. No wadded papers or discarded cans or even a single burnt cigarette end—no evidence at all that people had ever used the place.

It was late, then, and we started back. Ten minutes found us down again in the noise and press of the city, wondering if maybe we had only imagined such beauty. But we looked on a map afterward, and found that it really is there. The Parc de Saint-Cloud, it is called, and it must be one of the best-kept secrets of all of Paris. Otherwise the millions would have found their way to it, and there would be nothing left to tell.

Paris from the Parc de Saint-Cloud

16

B READ, OR *pain*, is masculine. But the long, thin loaf of it we buy every morning, called a *baguette*, is feminine. Don't ask me why. To someone from a backward country, where loaves do not contain the lascivious possibilities of gender, it is all deepest mystery.

Each day, for weeks, I would ask one of the girls behind the bakery counter of Prisunic for a *baguette*—using the masculine article, *un*—and her lip would curl in barely-containable disgust. Grudgingly she would draw it from the bin, choosing the smallest loaf she could find, fling it down on the counter, take my money and turn with relief to the next, more civilized customer.

Then, one morning, I heard the woman ahead of me in the line demand *une baguette*. Monkey hear, monkey do. The girls in the bakery department are noticeably more friendly, now that I have got the sex of the bread right. I understand this meticulousness about language, and I honor it. The spoken word is the oldest vessel of culture—the instrument by which peoples define and set themselves apart. Trifle with language and, in some way, you trifle with the nation.

But about the French attitude toward small change I am less forgiving.

When I first came to France—25 years ago, that's been—a dollar bought about four French francs. Memory may not be exact, but it was in that range. In other words, a franc was worth on the order of a quarter, in a time when a quarter was a significant coin. The latest currency quotation showed the franc at nearly 8.84 to the dollar, meaning that now, after time and inflation have debased the dollar itself, the basic French unit of exchange is worth 11.3 cents and weakening a fraction almost daily.

But the franc is not the least coin in use. There also is the 20-centime piece, worth 2.26 U.S. cents; the smaller 10-centime piece, worth slightly more than a penny, and finally the 5-centime coin, about the size of a shirt button, whose value can be expressed as $00.005658. What that will buy you in one of the most expensive cities on the planet can be left to the imagination.

These little brass centimes, in their various denominations, are nevertheless in daily circulation. Store clerks count them out with the change, as if they had real importance. What clerks do not like is to bother taking them back as tender for merchandise. I do not know what one is expected to do with them—hammer them into jewelry, or use them, like glass beads, for trade goods on future expeditions to the interior of Papua New Guinea. But they can hardly be spent, particularly the 10- and 5-centime pieces.

They accumulate first in the pocket and then, in larger heaps, on the bedside table. Eventually, in self-defense, they have to be dealt with. Either by opening an upper window and showering them with a wild cackle down into the street. Or, as a last resort, by trying to spend them.

Yesterday, after passing safely through the sexual minefield at the bread counter, I went around to the checkout stand to pay for a bottle of wine. A red table wine we like, unpedigreed but very agreeable, costs seven and one-half francs the bottle—or 85 cents at the current rate of exchange. Knowing this, I had counted out in advance 550 centimes in brassy bits and pieces. And since the store was practically empty, with all the checkers sitting idle at their registers, I laid this small change jingling before one of them, putting with it a larger 2-franc piece to make the amount correct.

She flew into an immediate rage. Whether out of simple laziness, or perhaps humiliation at the worthlessness of the coinage, I can't say. But she was furious, waving both hands at the pile as if to say *get it away*, she didn't want to count it.

Why not, I asked her. *C'est sans valeur?* It is valueless?

Her eyes blazed.

All right, if she didn't want to count it, I would. I had counted it once; I would do it again. When I finished, she hurled the centimes in her register with elaborate petulance. And as I walked away, she hissed something at me in the street vernacular that I do not yet understand in all its rich detail.

One's tolerance for rudeness finally wears thin. I turned and went the several steps back to her.

Listen, I told her, it's not *my* money—it's yours. Do you understand that? *C'est la monnaie française.*

But is it *la* or *le*, I wondered. What do you suppose is the sex of a 5-centime piece? Who really cares?

You know you have begun to feel at home when you are able to stand your ground.

17

LIVING IN A PLACE where people of so many wildly different sorts daily collide and mingle, one is struck by the extent to which the thing we call a culture is nothing more than the sum of our collective *agreements*. Probably that is a routine observation, but somehow it seems so much more apparent here.

The other day two young men from somewhere in middle Asia got aboard the métro and settled in the seat directly facing mine. If I write a lot about the métro, it is not out of any fascination with public transit but only because, unlike people seen passing on the street, one's fellow riders in the coach can be observed close at hand and for a longer time.

Anyway, these two young men sat down together and were

having a conversation in their native tongue. The strangest tongue it was, full of little trills and chirrups—quick, birdy noises of which you would not have thought the human mouth capable, and of course quite unintelligible to me. But these noises served them well, because they were having a hilarious good time, slapping their knees in merriment, teeth shining whitely in their brown faces as they laughed. After a while three other young men of the same origin boarded the coach, and those first two went to join them, all five united in temporary community by their agreement that the odd sounds they made constituted a language.

Two ladies from Indochina took the seats they'd vacated. Well-dressed, coming from shopping and carrying their parcels, they, too, had a lot to talk about—but in sounds that bore no relation to the ones just heard.

Behind them, standing by the door and waiting to get off at the next station, were some African men, speaking whichever of that continent's 800-odd tongues was agreed to be language by the people of their tribe or village. All around us in the car, meantime, were the ambient conversations of the French. And there sat I, trained by a lifetime's practice to make still different noises—ones that people in parts of the world would find pure gibberish.

Yet people are in many ways alike. From Borneo to Brussels, from the Cameroons to California, we are essentially the same creature, with a practically identical range of needs to make known, passions to cry out and ideas to express.

It is just that in diverging to populate the planet, at various times and in various places we invented different verbal symbols—none right, none wrong, all makeshift—to represent what was in our thoughts. The symbol itself is unimportant, since, in the accidental way of things, the word for love in one man's language could easily be the vilest oath in another's. That a critical number of us agree is all that matters, binding us together in distinct and workable groups.

Language is one such agreement, perhaps the principal one. But there are others.

Take fashion as an example. Among certain groups, high style once was thought to be achieved by various forms of elaborate self-mutilation. Among other groups, by wearing corsets and powdered wigs. And neither notion was intrinsically more ridiculous than the other.

Go to any museum here and notice the crowds. The people standing rapt before the paintings of the Impressionists and the older masters are almost exclusively western peoples. Their own antique landscapes are pictured there; their own faces look back at them from the canvases. The power of the paintings flows from an agreement as to what constitutes beauty. But other people are governed by different agreements. Their beauty may not be represented there.

These agreements extend to countless lesser matters. One group agrees that certain things are edible—insects, say, or snails or dogs. Another group counts the very idea of that repulsive. Or one group agrees that, when the bladder is distressed, the thing to do is simply to turn aside and relieve oneself against some public wall. While another group considers that bad form.

And, that, in the end, is what this thing is that we call a culture: the sum of all the agreements, large and small, of our particular group. Could it be that this is why, in almost every society, there is a certain bias against the outsider, the alien, who is not party to our agreements—who reminds us that there are many ways in the world to live, and that all these ways by which we feel at home within ourselves are only so much accidental nonsense after all?

18

Aɴʏ ʀᴇᴘᴏʀᴛᴇʀ ᴡᴏʀᴛʜ his keep would have at hand detailed information on the per capita volume of wine and spirits consumed annually by the French, the rate of alcoholism per 100,000 population, the yearly incidence of deaths from cirrhosis of the liver, the number of saloons per square kilometer in the Paris district and other such relevant data.

The numbers in all categories must be impressive. Surely those statistics are kept somewhere. Unfortunately, they do not seem to be in my notes. It's the symptomatology of the problem I find more interesting.

It is obvious from casual observation that public drunkenness is less a nuisance in France than in, say, either the Soviet Union or Poland, where intemperance—besides being a culturally learned behavior—is a necessary antidote to political despair. The French do not drink for the sullen purpose of forgetting who and where they are. They do not drink to numb themselves to their powerlessness against an oppressive or brutal regime, or to lessen a sense of tragedy at being Frenchmen alive in their time.

Oh, there are wrecks of human beings—ghastly, stinking heaps of rags—to be seen comatose on métro benches. But probably no more of them than you would find bedded most any cool night on the subway grates along the avenue outside the U.S. Department of State in Washington. Sometimes one of these will wake briefly from a stupor, open a crooked hole of a mouth and shriek some garbled craziness. But the others on the station platform do not notice—or seem not to. Then the train carries them safely on.

My impression is that the French drink so much and so constantly, mainly wine, for no worse reason than that it is so bountifully available. And because, by heaven, their wine is so *very good.*

A bottle of classy but not necessarily famous wine which, imported, would be priced at $10 or more on an American shelf, can be had in any store here for the equivalent of about $4. One wine we like is labeled only with a picture of a bunch of grapes and the words *Vin de Table de France* stamped in white paint directly on the glass. It is, as a connoisseur might say, uncomplicated. But it is clean-flavored and pleasing and costs well under a dollar. So who can say what a really *cheap* bottle might be had for?

Other segments of French agriculture are heavily subsidized, and perhaps the vineyards are as well. How well the price of wine reflects the real marketplace, or to what extent it is an expression of national priorities, I don't know.

I can only report that if, on the way back from the store with my bottle of *Vin de Table de France,* I happen to stop at a newsstand to pick up a couple of thin French daily newspapers, I will have paid nearly 20 cents more for the papers than I did for the wine. And for the price of having a jacket cleaned I can bring home my wine by the case.

Confronted by such a plenty, self-discipline is called for if one is not to be spoiled by a good thing and wind up a sad case.

In our building, for example, there is a man about my age—50 years or so—who leaves quite properly each morning, well-dressed in a suit and necktie, jaunty and clear-eyed as a hawk. And who then, at 9:30 every evening, with the punctuality of a railroad timekeeper, comes weaving home so smitten and befuddled that he cannot manage, unaided, the small manipulations necessary to unlock the building's door and find his way to bed. His powers of recovery are wonderful. But I give him about two more years before he is drooling and howling with the others on the métro benches.

That is how the wine of France, in all its abundance and goodness and modesty of price, can slip up on you. It is a long process, though, and insidious. And of course there are many lesser stages—slight stumblings, slurring, unintended repetitiveness and the like—that precede the visible collapse.

For example, in our building there is a man about my age who leaves quite properly each morning, well-dressed in a suit and necktie . . .

19

AT THE END of our block there is a miniature *étoile*, or star—a traffic circle with a garden of flowers and trees at its center and six streets entering at angles from the side. The largest of those streets, on which our building faces, if followed eastward plunges directly toward the heart of the city by way of connections either with the Rue Lecourbe or the Avenue Émile Zola. Or in the other direction, to west, it crosses the river to the suburb of Saint-Cloud and joins the autoroute to Malmaison, favorite residence of the young Napoleon and Joséphine, and on to the glory of Versailles.

But history is not the point of this. Traffic is. The six streets feeding into the circle carry, between them, 14 lanes of cars. The circle itself, however, can accommodate only three lanes. And there, as you may already suspect, is a problem.

Years ago I drove in Paris. And even then, when cars were fewer here, my hands for days afterward remained locked claw-like to the shape of the steering wheel, like the talons of a bird frozen to a wire. Today it would be several times more terrifying. As with football players who go soft in the off-season, even Parisians say that after summer holiday away from the city it takes them several days to get game-hardened again to the screech of tires, the sound of rent metal and the shock of contact.

Sitting at a sidewalk table of the café La Rotonde on the

perimeter of our circle and observing the *circulation,* as the French call all traffic, whether actually circular or deadly and straight, one comes to understand that the whole incredibly congested flow of people and machines is regulated less by signs and signals than by an elaborate system of subtle protocols.

Traffic lights, in fact, are all but meaningless. They are weakly illuminated and positioned for minimum visibility. And in any case they do not seem to carry any authority of law, giving at best an indefinite suggestion as to when something *might* happen—when pedestrians might attempt to cross, or when the cars might, with some small degree of probability, decide to stop. The lights are freely ignored. What appears to govern is the rule of right-hand precedence. That is, if the machine on the right can manage to get its near fender ahead of the machine on the left, it is entitled to proceed. On a circle with 14 lanes of traffic converging into three, the spatial relationships of all those fenders become complicated. Priority is gained or lost by measurements of centimeters.

As you would expect, misunderstandings are fairly common. At the auto repair shop a little way down our street, heaped at the curb for each Monday's collection, is the proof—the twisted bumpers and mangled door panels—of what happens when someone out there in the maelstrom blinks or loses his nerve.

Pedestrian crossing signals are given even less weight. People stride out into traffic when it pleases them to. Babies being pushed in carriages are deferred to. Or let some tawny young thing is designer jeans and spike heels step deliberately off the curb, tossing the onrushing drivers a charming *moue,* and they hit their brakes gladly. But do that same thing accidentally in lumpish middle age and you had better have your affairs in order.

The insanity is compounded by the mix of machines, from bicycles and mopeds and 3-wheeled motorized boxes evolving toward being cars, to cars proper and buses and rumbling

Careful crossing

trucks. One morning at our corner a car and a motorcycle—the driver of one of them evidently watching the wrong fender—met unfortunately. The cyclist was staggering dazed in the intersection. A crowd gathered, reassembled the detached parts of his machine, collected up the cargo of boxes he had been carrying behind, lashed them back on, and the cyclist, finding himself still alive, set forth again.

The next day, same hour and same intersection, the casualty was a woman on a pedal bike. Again the result was not tragic. Bystanders brushed her off and, pushing her disabled bicycle, she disappeared limping up a side street. Such small encounters are so routine that the names and addresses of the participants were not even exchanged.

But there must be worse. Because intermittently through the day and on into night ambulances rush up and down our street with their strange sirens going *WOOOO-ahh WOOOO-ahh,* crying out the announcement of what happens, in spite of protocols, where 14 lanes turn into three.

20

IT IS A CONCERT HALL whose acoustics are incredible but whose audience is hard to hold. It also is a bazaar, a den of thieves, an unofficial social agency, a flower shop, a public urinal, a bedding place for the homeless, an asylum for the harmlessly deranged, a fashion show, a political stage, a stink, a rush of wind.

Last, and almost incidentally, it is a means of transport, the system of hidden arteries through which the city's lifeblood flows. It is the Paris métro—the 29-cent ride to anywhere in town, and the ticket to endless entertainment. Guide books and tour agencies suggest itineraries for visiting the city's landmarks, as well they should. The métro is mentioned as one way to get about. But the métro is not only to be used. It has to be *experienced* as a wonder in its own right. Anyone who misses that will have left without quite knowing Paris.

Performances are forbidden. But the nearly 300 station platforms, the thousands of train cars, the miles of buried corridors, are far too many to police. Officialdom throws up its hands in hopelessness, and the show goes on.

The accordion player, a man in his 60s, stations himself regularly in a passageway just down from the Condorde stop. He is there faithfully as someone punching a clock. It is his job. Standing gray and very erect, he sends out his music—a waltz or a lullaby, some relic of another age—that people carry away humming as they rush to their next connection. He has the bearing of nobility fallen on lean times, and his eyes are far away, lost in memories or the music. He never looks at the coins the people drop into his open instrument case.

Around a corner, in the correspondence tunnel to a different line, there sat one day on a stool, her music stand before her, a blonde young woman in a flowered dress, swaying as she evoked from her cello the most accomplished melodies. And the combination—just at that point in the labyrinth where the music of accordion and cello faintly met—was strangely pleasing.

In another passage farther along the No. 1 main east-west line, at Châtelet it may have been, four Senegalese drummers, squatting over their kettles and stretched hides, generated a rhythmically complicated thunder that was violent as the storms of Africa itself—swelling, pulsing, spreading out through the resonating network of passages like some threat of apocalypse, almost stopping the walkers in their tracks.

The instruments are as varied as the talents, which may be prodigious or slight. Flute players, pallid and serene. Boys blowing bug-eyed into harmonicas. Men with small electric pianos and synthesizers. Puckered Orientals with Fu-Manchu mustaches, sitting cross-legged, plucking curious homemade contraptions of boxes and strings to produce thin, doleful notes that are music only to their ears.

One moment you are riding a quiet coach from Palais Royal on the southbound No. 7 line, the only sound the chatter of the wheels. The next moment an energetic gang of boys and girls has leapt aboard, with portable amplifiers, and begun a medley of nicely-polished folk songs. By the time the train has gotten to Jussieu, several stops further along, the act is finished and coins—small ones, and not many of them—have jingled into the leather purse that one of the musicians passes.

Maybe the singers will someday be discovered, or maybe they are happy working the trains. They leap off again with their paraphernalia and, a stop later, a sad-looking young Spaniard takes their place. Probably he was the best guitar player in his village somewhere, and came to Paris to make a big success. But he found the city full of ones like him, and he has to eat. His fingers race over the strings but no one appears to listen.

And after him, maybe it will be the hand-puppeteer. From the front of the car comes a sudden explosion of calliope music. Quicker than the telling, someone has strung a black curtain between two posts, and above the curtain's top a pair of woolly creatures is engaged in some argument over a straw flower. The riders turn in their seats to watch. They laugh.

Parisians are wooden-faced on the métro. It is just their manner. They never smile, at strangers or at one another. That anyone could make them actually *laugh* is nearly unimaginable. The puppet drama moves from envy and rage to reconciliation. The two creatures decide to share the flower. The music ends, the curtain comes down, the people feel in their pockets for a coin. And, quickly as he came, the puppeteer is gone.

So it repeats, endlessly, every day, on every line.

Between these there are vendors selling overripe avocados. Or bargain roses, dew-sparkling and wrapped in cellophane,

Métro at Porte Dauphine

that wilt as soon as they pass to the buyer's hand. Or other produce whose blemishes are less noticeable in the subterranean light.

There are places, if you are hungry, to buy food of the hasty, stand-up kind. And just in the next corridor from the snack stall, you can be sure, there will be beggars propped against the wall with empty purses outstretched. Or others hunkered on the floor, heads between their knees in despair or shame, with elaborate hand-lettered signs explaining in detail the reasons for their desperate circumstances or the keenness of their hunger. And if your own food is still unfinished in your hand, perhaps you drop some centimes in the box.

There are young Iranian exiles carrying signs that say "Khomeini Executes Pregnant Women" and collecting signatures against the outrages in their homeland. There are imitation Boy Georges and strutting punk queens in spangled capes and pastel-colored mohawks, trying desperately to attract attention in a city where Godiva herself naked on horseback might pass quite unremarked.

There are winos curled up asleep with their empty bottles, and lunatics of all ages and races and descriptions wandering wild-eyed and all-but-unnoticed through the multitudes, screeching complaints and revelations.

And always, everywhere, there are the Gypsy pickpockets waiting to relieve you of wallet and passport at any careless moment, either on the station platform or in a crowded car.

But above all there is the sense of all those millions of Parisians streaming out in the morning about their day's business, and then, in the evening, when the jammed coaches fill up with the smoke of tired bodies not lately washed, all going home again. Also, perhaps, one gets some insight into the nature of great cities everywhere, where some live well and others live on the leavings. Although considering the number of marginal people in the métro's hidden world, the leavings must in the aggregate be prodigious.

The other day I met three young men with guitars in a bar outside a métro station, where they'd stopped to rest and drink a beer and count their coins before going back down to play the afternoon rush. They arranged their earnings—mostly little brass centime pieces—in equal stacks on the table, and then divided those.

They'd been working the No. 6 line, they said, from Étoile to Nation, playing and singing for five stops, then passing their purse and getting off to wait for the next train. Sometimes they got nothing for their trouble. But on the average, they said, their take was about 14 francs each half-hour, counting the time between trains and the getting on and off. For a 10-hour day of playing, that came to a few cents more than $10 apiece.

And even in Paris, if you have a little talent and a world of energy and are careful with your money, that's a life.

21

THE EAVE TROUGHS of Prague, on an inclement day, drip tears of bitter memory. London, when the weather closes down, can be ponderous in shades of gray and black. But Paris is never sad or sullen in a rain.

A churning, painter's sky rolls up behind the old turrets and spires, giving artistic importance to the moment. The first drops tap against awning or window glass. Umbrellas unfold like a thousand bravely-colored rain flowers, and the gaiety goes on. For every sidewalk café that fronts upon the wetness there will be three others, somewhere, facing cozily away. The people rearrange themselves. The exposed tables empty, the dry ones fill up. And not one less cognac or coffee is drunk.

Only the 3-day tourists, interrupted on their rounds of scenic marvels, resent the weather. They console themselves by surging back and forth like cornered bison under the sidewalk arcade of the Rue de Rivoli, where their frenzy of buying makes the merchants rich. The Rue de Rivoli can be very pleasant at 10 o'clock on a dry morning, but it is a place to stay clear of in a rain.

Today was wet almost from daylight onward. Freshets tumbling in every street gutter carried a week's litter away, and then ran clear. The domes on the upper building corners glistened shiny-fat. The air was as nearly country clean as the air of a great city is ever apt to be.

We took our coffee outdoors, under the awning on the sheltered side of the café on the circle at the end of our street, and watched the people pass. Many went coatless and seemed indifferent to the certainty of getting wet. Afterward, having an errand in that direction, we thought we might spend part of an hour in the Jeu de Paume museum. The paintings there—the Degas, Monets, Renoirs, Cézannes and all that glorious company—are ones you like to revisit often. It would have been interesting to look with a particular eye, on such a day as this one, at how artists saw Paris in rainy light.

But the museum was closed early. There had been an unpleasant telephone call, and people had been asked to leave. A clutch of blue-uniformed police blocked the door while their colleagues inside searched the place for a bomb. Someone, it seems—some nickel-and-dime terrorist from some 49-cent republic somewhere—had tried to dignify his grubby cause by threatening to blow up a few of civilization's treasures.

To the primitive ear, the noise of an explosion is a fully-satisfying political statement.

So we walked through the Tuileries instead, our umbrella folded, getting sprinkled and showered upon by turns, and the garden was lovelier than we'd seen it before—the wet gravel walkways quiet underfoot, the statues washed a new white, the trees so astonishingly green that they seemed almost to be lighted from within. Empty of people, the place was oddly more hospitable and less formal, not so much a sculpted artifact as something alive and suited to this time. At the pool at the far end, a woman was feeding bits of bread to enormous carp that swirled the rain-stippled water as they rose, white-mouthed, to take the pieces from her hand.

Wet ourselves, then, my wife and I came home. In Paris, such small things can wonderfully fill a rainy day.

Just at evening's end, the sky abruptly cleared. The clouds all rushed away to southeastward, leaving not a scrap of themselves behind. Blue light paled to lemon beyond the river, and then went out. Now the sky is full of stars and outside the window hangs half a moon, promising a fine tomorrow.

The Jeu de Paume did not blow up after all, culture having survived craziness one more day. The city and the night have a washed sharpness. After the rain, it is October in August, again.

22

THE BUILDINGS ARE mostly old, the trees and statues and all the layered memories old. Yet every day is new. Nothing is static; all is in motion. And that is the special wonder of this city: the endlessly unexpected as a counterpoint to the everlastingly known.

The other morning early, out of anything to smoke and setting forth on the widening search for an open *tabac* among all the ones closed for the month, I found a gendarme positioned watchfully at every corner along the street. Were the traffic signals out of order? No, for whatever slight notice anyone ever pays them, they seemed to be winking normally through their cycles. Was there perhaps some public disorder expected, then? The newspaper had made no mention of anything like that.

From beyond our traffic circle, in the direction of the river, there arose a distant commotion—horns blaring, sirens *WOOOOahh*-ing, the racket of a great many engines. And then, while the foot officers blocked the side streets, there came rushing around the circle and on past a sudden convoy: a squad of motorcycle police in proud formation, official looking cars, a regular cavalcade of wheeled machines all in a self-important hurry.

And after that came the bicyclists. Far out ahead was the apparent leader, bent low over his handlebars and pumping furiously, flanked by more men on motorcycles. Behind him there was a considerable space of a block or more. And then the pack, half a hundred men at least, bunched close. The only sounds as they passed were their drawn breaths and the hiss of their tires on the pavement, like wind hurrying through leaves. After them, separated by perhaps another block, came a few laggards, open-mouthed and sweating at their work. And still farther back—minutes back—one rider by himself, weaving a little. And behind him a fleet of ambulances.

No Tour de France, this, with fame as the prize and legions lining the way to hail the riders on. It was some local event only, but done with full official pageantry. Quickly it came and went in the morning's shaded coolness, and traffic began crossing again. But the gendarmes stayed at their corners.

I found tobacco and came back and finished looking at the newspaper, and had just made coffee and sat to work when the whole spectacle was repeated—the sirens, the roar of engines, the windy rush of bikes. There's no saying what race it was or where it began or ended. But each lap of the course was exactly 45 minutes long, because that was the time it took the riders to come back around and pass under the window, not just a second time but even, finally, a third, the main field still bunched but with the stragglers and ambulances farther behind.

Then came a woman pedaling alone, her bicycle's wire basket full of bread. The police went away. But immediately some men came with trucks and set up a market along the street—an extensive open-air market stretching the whole length of the block, fat with country things grown somewhere close by and brought to town for selling. By middle afternoon, men and trucks and produce were gone again.

Like slides changing in a projector—empty morning street, bike race, farmers' market, street empty once more—everything happened with amazing suddenness, giving to the day a mood of rich improvisation.

It brought to mind those African trinket-sellers you find in good weather on the hill of Montmartre, on the steep sidewalks leading up to the Sacré-Coeur church. Desert-lean, angular in their white robes, they squat behind spread blankets on which their wares of cheap jewelry and other gew-gaws are invitingly displayed. One moment they are there. Then, perhaps spying the distant glint of authority's badge, they rise as one all over the hill—communicating by some signal too slight to be seen, so that it seems telepathic—and snatch up their blankets by the corners in jingling bundles and are gone as quickly as birds.

Presently the alarm, whatever it was, passes. Then you look again and, as if by further magic, they are back, blankets spread and wares all perfectly arranged.

That is how this city shows herself. You just wake up here and open yourself to each day, and wait to see what it will bring.

23

THE DRESSMAKER'S CAT, gray tabby, sleeps among the buttons and threads and scraps of lace on a window shelf facing the street, sole tenant and guardian after hours, waking when the sun slips down behind the buildings to look out through the dusty glass at people hurrying up the Rue de Silly with their loaves of weekend bread. She has nowhere to hurry to, the dressmaker's cat—just dreams two days away until the weekend passes and the people's bread is eaten. Then a key turns in the lock and she can feel a hand again.

The saloon cat, glossy black, lives among the legs of wine-drinkers in the *brasserie* near the end of the bridge of Bir-Hakeim, just down from the Eiffel Tower—fattens on the bits that careless fingers drop, and on any creeping thing by name of mouse or larger that dares come out of the gutter pipe or up the cellar drain. Ventures only as far as the open door, sometimes, and sits surveying the smoke and noise and danger of the wheels. Then goes gladly back to live among the legs.

Each morning at half past 8, the white apartment cat comes out onto a ledge no wider than a hand laid flat, and follows that along the building front to the next window and crouches, peering in. What he sees there must be wonderful. It would have to be, to be worth making that walk for. The ledge is 10 floors above the street. Turning is impossible, so he goes carefully backward the way he came, interested in the pigeons but disciplined when they dart close, understanding perfectly the risks, doing nothing ill-considered, that cat, and staying only a short time before he is back at his own window where arms lift him in. How long would it take on a 5-inch, 10th-floor ledge to get anybody wide-awake and started on the day?

In a side courtyard of the Cathedral of Notre-Dame, the antiquarian cats ghost mottled and sharp-ribbed between the

The saloon cat

The dressmaker's cat

fallen stones of glory in relentless decay. Eight hundred years ago some of those stones were cut and nothing—no empire or conceit of man—is meant to stand that long. Fallen pieces are carried to the courtyard to be saved and put back as time permits, if not in this century then perhaps the next. The cats of Notre-Dame, an ancient line, snarl and mate and bear their careless litters amid broken cornice parts and the grinning heads of gargoyles.

And finally, our cat, whose life will be the longest, frowns out with amber statuary eyes through the leaves of a potted plant, perfectly content although his perspective never changes, not really needing the touch of any hand or even the company of his kind. But nevertheless watching the rooftops just to see if any of these others he knows might pass.

24

INCONVENIENCED BY SO MANY closed shops, and envious of all those Parisians fled away to pleasure somewhere in the country, we have finally hired a car and pointed it along the road to see where everyone has gone.

Half of them appear to have gone to Versailles to wait in 2-hour lines outside the palace, and afterward to circulate along the gravel walkways of the vast grounds, getting rocks in their shoes. The other half, give or take a million, have gone farther south, to the region of the Loire, to watch the tour buses unload. There are rumors of people going other places—west to the Brittany coast or down to the Riviera or the Mediterranean island of Corsica—but I cannot vouch for that. Suffice that there are enough people at Versailles and one or two of the other major attractions to fill a city of any size.

Of course, not all in these ambulatory masses are French. The great courtyard of Versailles, for example, we found to be populous with Japanese tourists, all following purposefully, politely, in close-pressed groups behind guides with upraised umbrellas, halting from time to time to take pictures of each other taking pictures of each other or of the palace. The sound of their Nikon lenses opening and shutting was like a tireless breeze.

Farther south, in château country, Germans are the dominant tribe. As you drive up the gentle valley of the River Cher from Montrichard and turn off the road down a majestic avenue of ancient plane trees toward the castle of Chenonceaux, the first view is enough to take your breath away. I do not speak of the château itself, which cannot yet be seen, but rather of the *champs de voitures*—the imposing fields of parked vehicles spreading away on either side of the trees.

Above all the other machines arrayed in those lots, the tour buses loom like whales in a sea of herring. And most of them are of German registry. They have come south and crossed the Rhine and struck to the heart of France, just as yesterday's armies came. Out of them bounds a company, a brigade, a veritable *wehrmacht* of energetic Aryans, all whooping and ruddy and heavy-footed, grinning with wonderful teeth, seeming likely at almost any moment to break into an anthem of militant and boundless well-being. All sizes, these Germans are. Big ones, followed by straw-haired, blue-eyed miniatures of themselves, the small ones impatient to grow up and have lederhosen of their own and go tromping and talking loudly across Europe in their turn.

The German buses are parked in perfect rows, like tanks lined up for inspection. The drivers polish them with towels while the German tourists lope off after their *führer*—meaning "leader," whether of tours or bigger enterprises—to buy another five dozen postcards. When such a group passes noisily by, a silence seems to fall. Maybe I only imagine it, but my impression is that the French avoid noticing them in the same deliberate way one ignores something unfortunate on the sidewalk.

You wonder if the tour agencies in Frankfurt and Karlsruhe and Bonn include on the itinerary any stops at French villages martyred in the war. It has been 40 years, now. Many of these visiting Germans were not alive then. Some were, but many not. The question, though, is more complicated than just history. It has to do with temperament—with the restless and somehow fearsome vitality of these ruddy people pouring stridently out of their buses to conquer the next touristic objective.

One reads in the newspapers now of tentative moves toward rapprochement by the two Germanys, east and west, and also of Russian nervousness at the very thought—however remote the chance—that these divided energies might be unwholesomely recombined. But, if truth be told, who *anywhere in Europe* really wants the Germans reunited? They travel well, spend freely, leave many *Deutschmarks* behind. They are good for the economy, and yet . . .

We have stopped tonight in the town of Loches. The hotels are full, but we have found rooms in an *auberge*, with bathroom in the hall and tavern and restaurant below. The window looks across a medieval village, with house walls leaning and no roof comb straight, and down into a lane just wide enough for two horse carts to pass. On the hill at the town's center is the château in whose hall the maid of Orléans, Joan, came to persuade the weakling Charles to claim his crown as the ruler of all France. And in the château's dungeons, which we will visit tomorrow, are chambers where the shrieks of the tortured may still echo in the mind. So perhaps no country of Europe is without its history of horrors.

But only one of them was monstrous in our time.

25

THERE IS A LIMIT to the mind's absorptive powers in visiting châteaux. No two travelers' capacities are the same, but for each there is some level of satiety which, when surpassed, causes one turret or battlement or stagnant moat to look a good deal like all the rest.

The architectural vanity of several centuries of French royalty was truly prodigious. The castles they commanded to be built reveal a vaulting self-estimation, although from their portraits that still hang on some of the walls many of these noble landlords can be seen to have been weak and venal and altogether ordinary characters.

But they were tireless contractors, I will give them that. The hills that border the valley of the Loire and its nearby tributaries are honeycombed with tunnels where men once toiled in smoking torchlight gloom, quarrying the blocks of soft, white limestone to construct the fortresses and stately homes. Architects and artists were imported from Italy—from anywhere in Europe. Expense was no object. It never is, when indulgence can be financed by mulcting the lesser classes. So the stone-cutters cut and the peasants tilled and tithed. And the royalty built these castles for themselves, as monuments against that day when, in history's inevitable squaring of accounts, the people would come to take off their heads.

There are said to be 1,000 châteaux in the Loire region. In the past two days we have seen 700 or 800 of them. I haven't counted, but it seems at least that many.

My wife's absorptive limit was reached in the dungeons of Loches, while inspecting graffiti scratched into the stone—in the single spot illuminated by a ray of sunlight through a wall slit—by some wretch who spent years in that dank and awful place, perhaps for coming up a bushel short at rent time. My own limit was achieved at Azay-le-Rideau, when a woman went gray-faced in the press of the crowd and had to be supported to a window to keep from fainting, and I realized that if we had to look at one more tapestry or pair of crossed battle axes none of us might make it out of there alive.

No doubt our lack of staying power cost us other opportunities. At the château of Cheverny, for instance—which is set in a hunting forest and reported to be still partly lived in—we could have gone on the tour and had shown to us the 6,000-year-old horns of the giant ancestral stag. We decided to take their word for it, and sat outside the wall in a café instead. By day's end we had reduced our inspections of châteaux to a quick swing up the drive in the car, a paragraph read aloud from the guide book, and an immediate retreat to the road. The magnificence of the French gentry was passing in a dutiful but painless blur.

Tonight we are done with looking at castles. Tonight we are *in one*, having made a dazzling social ascent from a cramped room over the saloon in the auberge at Loches to cushier quarters in the Château de Pray just outside Amboise.

Our window looks down into a charming courtyard. Our daughters' chamber is in the castle tower itself, looking over the terrace and the flowered grounds, down a gentle slant of countryside to the sandbars and braided channels of the Loire. Tables have been laid for dinner on the terrace, with crisp blue linen and silver and crystal and Limoges china. Soon, as the evening lengthens, the white-coated waiters will take up their stations beside the wall. And we will go down with the others to drink and eat in the cool air, watching mist collect between the hills on the far side of the river.

Briefly we are living as the nobles did, though rather more conveniently. I have to admit that it is not so bad. And the cost, though steep, will be less than our heads. But for us, even as for them, all good things end.

My favorite château story is of that titled Frenchman who

completed his castle at huge expense, gave an ostentatious party for thousands, serving his guests—the king among them—on golden plates. Whereupon the king, furious at being upstaged, confiscated the fellow's château and fortune and clapped him in prison for the rest of his life.

That abruptly, when we have paid tomorrow's bill, will we return to the real world.

26

THE ROAD NORTH from Orléans toward Paris mounts up from the river valley past the last woodlands of the Loire, then proceeds across a vast tableland where grain elevators and church steeples mark the separated villages, as on the American plain, and where the trembling poplars that border the asphalt are almost the only trees to be seen.

That stretch of country, as we passed through it, was colored an endless brown-gold of ripe wheat. Distances were lost in haze. In the immensity of the spreading fields, the harvest was just beginning, a full six weeks after the crop of the central United States had been gotten in. Fat and uniform, those fields were, and clean-harvested where the machines had passed. They were the fields of farming cooperatives. Sometimes four big combine harvesters could be seen passing across them abreast, with trucks or tractors and wagons following to receive the threshed grain. The country's appetite for bread is great, its weather favorable. Clearly the French have become experts at growing wheat.

We turned off the highway and down a grassy lane between two fields. The lane formerly had crossed a railroad track, but with the coming of express trains the way had been permanently barricaded and the abandoned house of the crossing-keeper had sunk into roofless decay.

We found a lone tree, a rare amenity in all that openness, and arranging ourselves in its slight shade got out our picnic provisions—bread, smoked meat, wine, a thick slice of mild cheese and a bag of small, sweet peaches bought from a woman with a stand at an orchard's edge. And it was there, while we were eating, that one of our daughters spoke for the first time of *home*.

The mind, the heart, are wonderfully adaptable. They make investments in a place, and wrap themselves in its familiarity. Then, when necessity commands, they put it behind and begin the process again. And the capacity for these investments is seemingly unending.

Thus it was not some home an ocean away of which she spoke now. But rather the one just at the end of the road along which our car was pointed: a rented lodging, in a city that not many weeks ago was utterly strange, on a street where the several languages spoken do not include our own. Yet *home* was what she called it. And as always, when a journey is finished except for the last work of travel itself, we all yearned to be there.

So, packing up the remains of lunch, we sped out of the lane and north again along the highway. The traffic coming into the city was less fierce than we expected. We found our way, our building, and—thanks to all those still-absent Parisians—even a place to park.

I sank into one of the leather chairs of Monsieur Demeulen-aere, the landlord, and no chair ever fit me better. In fact, the rooms and all their furnishings—about which I made some snide comments at the start—seemed wonderfully companionable. I find it hard, now, to imagine living any other place, or rising daily to the view from any other window.

In short, our hearts are settled here.

Monsieur Demeulenaere himself is back on leave from Egypt. That is, he came back briefly, telephoned to ask how we were settled, then rushed away again with his family for holiday in Austria. On the phone he sounded like a young man, humorous and very nice. In a few days, when he has returned from the mountains but before going back out to Cairo, he promises to stop by for a visit in his home and mine.

I will mention to him then about the broken faucet handle in the bathroom and the dripping water leak from the front of the refrigerator. But after this necessary small business is concluded between us, I suspect I am going to like him, after all.

27

THE MONGRELIZATION OF France is so far advanced as to be almost surely irreversible. I am not speaking of the society itself. What happens in French bedrooms, and between whom, is a purely private matter. I am speaking of the society's dogs.

That a nation so thornily defensive of its culture, so meticulous about language, so finicky about the pedigrees of its wines should be so irresponsible about the propagation of its dogs seems strangely out of character.

One of our entertainments on a fine afternoon is to sit at an outside table at the café on the circle of our street and watch people go by with dogs on leashes. The creatures do not paw the pavement and lunge at the end of the lead, as any dog of mine would. They seldom bark. They never go raging off, dragging the owner behind, to chase a cat or enjoy a good fight. A bit spiritless, these dogs may be, but unfailingly well-mannered. They march discreetly at heel. Their masters and mistresses never need to whistle or cajole or bawl furious commands. They simply make their wishes known in a conversational murmur and the dogs, evidently fluent in the comprehension of French, if not yet in the speaking of it, instantly obey.

It is a model of reciprocal consideration, this relationship. When passing along a sidewalk, the people stop often and willingly to allow the sniffing of trees and lamp posts so that their charges may detect who else of the neighborhood has recently come that way. They wait, without embarrassment, as other necessary duties are performed. They take their dogs on the métro, where the animals sit quietly, waiting to be notified that the proper stop is near. They take them into grocery stores, the hair salon, the tavern—even into the restaurant. And the dogs honor this great trust by neither whining for table scraps nor fouling the waiter's trouser leg as he is serving the *entrecôte* of veal or lobster in cream.

I have told all the good I could think of first, saving the bad for last. The other side of the coin is their appearance. You think of France, and you imagine a nation of poodles. And you are wrong.

Most of these dogs that go by on leashes are mongrels of the most wildly improbable mixes and shapes. Sometimes it is possible to detect—or at least make some rough guess about—the remote ancestral lines, to imagine where such a beast might have come from. But it's hopeless to try to say what it is now, or where, in the shuffling of the genetic deck, it might be headed.

Yesterday a man came past our café table with something monstrous on the end of a cord. It appeared to be a cross between a German shepherd and a basset—not so terrible in the abstract, except that the two breeds had transmitted their characteristics unaltered. Thus this creature was, in its upper parts, a full-sized police dog—heavy, muscular body, great head with pricked ears and gaping, toothy jaws, a wolfish tail. A powerful example of the breed. This superstructure, however, was supported on five-inch legs with splayed basset feet, the feet and the tiny legs moving in a blur to propel the upper bulk along. So that the impression somehow was of a hairy, fanged, overweight centipede scuttling at the end of a leash.

And there are ones even more awful. Bulldogs mated with whippets, giving issue to creatures with the face of one and the body of the other. Things that started out to be wiener dogs, but decided midway to be terriers instead. Scotties as big as Labrador retrievers. Beagles standing waist-high on legs like wolfhounds'. Dogs that look like anteaters. Tiny, bug-eyed dogs as hairless and pale as cave rats. All of them are well-loved, well-leashed, always under perfect control. So it is inconceivable—and this is the worst part—that their couplings could be accidental. They must be the product of some national French experiment to find the perfect dog.

Apartment dwellers, all these creatures are. Between their morning and evening promenades, they are confined in the building while their owners sleep or go away for the day to work somewhere in the city. Any breeder of livestock can tell you the dangers of selecting for one characteristic alone. But what the French are looking for, I believe—never mind the aesthetics—is an animal with an infinite capacity of bladder.

Fiddle with Mendel and you get what you deserve.

28

FROM THE RELENTLESS police inspector, Javert, in Victor Hugo's masterpiece, *Les Misérables,* to Agatha Christie's unraveler of murderous knots, Hercule Poirot, French detectives have basked in a fictional reputation of infallibility. If one of them was on your trail, no sewer could hide you, no scheme save you. But I think it is just that, a *fiction.*

It may be that, unknown to me or anyone else in Paris, great works of police detection are being accomplished daily. If so, reports of them are not to be found in the newspapers and therefore escape general notice. My observation of the Paris police is that, aside from blocking off streets for parades and bicycle races, what they do best is ride around four together in a small car, looking cramped but natty in their blue uniforms and little pillbox hats, getting out once in a while to impress their authority on someone who may have violated some obscure regulation but who plainly presents no public danger.

This view may be—no doubt is—colored by the fact that the Gypsies have struck again.

Once burned, I am now the soul of caution. Anything I don't want taken I keep in an inner pocket, with my hand around it. But my wife came to town several weeks after me, an innocent. Three little Gypsy girls, no older than our own daughters, found her in a block-long line outside a museum. And blowing kisses, waving a paper in her face for distraction, took her money—luckily, not a lot of it—directly from her hand with such skill that she didn't know for several moments she'd lost anything. Skipping merrily, still blowing kisses, the three little thieves vanished over the quay's edge down to the river. And naturally, through all of this or after, no policeman was to be seen.

This plague of "finger artists," as they're sometimes called, is said to be worse this year than most, so bad, in fact, that the city distributed pamphlets and posted signs telling how to keep your valuables from being lifted. Who has lost how much, and by what ruse, is a dominant topic among tourists waiting in line at the central post office to send home letters and picture postcards saying how much fun they're having in Paris. Like me, even when talking to each other, they all keep one hand in their pockets.

Apartment robberies also are a perennial problem, especially in the vacation season. According to Madame Freguin, the concierge, there have been no fewer than eight in our building in recent weeks, including the robbery of Monsieur Farchakh, our neighbor on this floor. But no policeman has been in evidence anywhere about. And now the track has gotten cold, even for a Hercule Poirot.

The police are busy, as far as I can tell, with other, bigger stuff. We saw them assemble in force one night to roust a single street magician off a corner near the Place Saint-Michel in the Latin Quarter. The pedestrians were unhappy, but the men in uniform seemed proud to have nipped crime in the bud. Much effort also goes into silencing the musicians who play in the métro tunnels, giving unauthorized pleasure to the riders of the trains. It can't be done, but it is intermittently attempted.

The African trinket-vendors require special vigilance. Chased off the butte of Montmartre, they are apt to reassemble at Place Trocadéro or under the Eiffel Tower, as they had one afternoon when we were passing that way. Suddenly they all rose up, gathered their goods in blanket bundles, and vanished quick as deer through a narrow park and into the labyrinth of the city. Presently the police came running in hot pursuit, sweating and portly some of them, slapping their pistol holsters, blundering into one fenced-off cul-de-sac after another, cursing in embarrassment. After that they rode around a while in cars of four. And finally, in frustration, piled out again to chase away a young North African man with a charcoal grate who proposed to offend civil order by selling passers-by something tasty to eat.

My own single, direct encounter was in a park—the one on the hill in Saint-Cloud where we have several times taken picnics. Our cloth was spread on the grass in the shade of a tree, and we had just finished eating and begun to pack our basket when a policeman came out of the far bushes and strode toward us with a stern look, calling out something about the *pelouse*. A *pelouse* is a lawn, or any grassy area, and the ones in France, even in parks, or maybe especially in parks, are only for looking at. They are not to be trod on, much less picnicked on.

The policeman was small and stout, with a round face and a little waxed mustache that fairly twitched at our effrontery. I mumbled some obsequities in English, and pretended not to understand his French, which mostly I didn't. And we made a hasty and humble show of getting out of there, thus avoiding a fine or worse.

When what I really longed to do was to throw up my hands and cry out to him, "Javert, you sly devil, you've caught up with me at last!"

29

DESPITE THEIR APARTMENT being robbed, our neighbors the Farchakhs did go away on holiday to Lebanon, after all. They are back now. And the other afternoon, when we returned from some small excursion, we found a note slipped under our door. Seeing as their good friends (and our landlords), the Demeulenaeres, would be in Paris for several days before going out again to Egypt, the note said, perhaps we would be free to come next door for dinner, *ensemble,* at 8 o'clock the next evening.

Of course we were free. Almost every night is free here. And a fine evening it was.

Lebanese hospitality is at once warmly informal and relentlessly generous. I have not been in that country since before the interminable war came to rain death and ruin and to destroy, certainly for our lifetimes and perhaps for all time, Lebanon's sun-washed but fragile civility. And I was struck anew by how undeserving are those people of the catastrophe into which the greed and rage of others has plunged them.

It turns out that George Farchakh is a colleague, a journalist. Or was until, not many years ago, I suspect worn out from writing about a tragedy without change or end, he came to Paris and went into the business of translation. His wife, Salma, also is a translator, and both are trilingual in Arabic, English and French.

Georges poured drinks around. Then the Demeulenaeres arrived—our *propriétaires*. And, yes, after having gotten past my first uncomfortable sense of trespass in their home, we found them immediately charming. They are in their middle 30s, the Farchakhs a few years older. Madame Demeulenaere also is Lebanese—a handsome and opinionated woman. Her husband, Marc, though French, grew up there. He is slender, athletic-looking and genial, though quieter than his wife, perhaps a bit shy or only self-contained. He is a banker, and has gone out from Paris to his company's Cairo branch for three years, where he is attempting to introduce computers to an Egyptian staff whose preference still is for 19th-century, desk-sized multi-columned ledgers.

We told them how happily settled we are in their apartment. And they were pleased by that, because it is not just a property they keep for rent. It is their home, to which they'll sometime come back. More drinks were poured. And Georges took up the conversation where we had left it when the Demeulenaeres arrived.

Who did the Lebanese blame for their disaster? I had asked him earlier. *Was the United States at fault?*

"As for your question," Georges said now—and he repeated it for the others. "The answer is yes. I am sorry, but since you ask—yes. And the reason is that your country does not have a policy in the Middle East. You support Israel. But support for one party or another is not a policy.

"And then, after President Reagan made so many promises to the president of Lebanon, your ship came to take your soldiers away. It is one thing if the promises had never been made. Maybe then Gemayal would not have felt so strong. Maybe he would have been more willing to make compromises. Perhaps something could have been saved. But the promises were made, and then the ship took the soldiers away. The promises meant nothing. Do you know what the Lebanese call your ship, the New Jersey?"

He looked at the others who nodded, knowing already.

"In Arabic," Georges said, "the word for shame is very close to the sound of *Jersey*. So that's what they call your ship now, the *New Shame*."

His words struck resonances of a conversation I had, 14 years ago this month, with a Lebanese man prominent in his country's affairs, at his home on a mountainside outside Beirut. *"You are doomed to be implicated in this part of the world,"* he had said. *"But you cannot dabble. The point is to be implicated with a result."* A long time ago, that was, when it was still thought that Lebanon might escape the maelstrom. Now, after an eternity of dabbling, the country is destroyed.

The Farchakh table groaned with good things that followed one another in long succession. And as the conversation plunged on, with voices sometimes raised in one or another of three languages, my wife, the peacemaker, tried to steer the talk onto less contentious ground. It didn't work. The life of that part of the world turns on discussion, on argument, and the argument will never be finished. But the Lebanese are masters at separating people from the blunders of governments. So, after the Turkish coffee had been drunk, there was no rancor, only friendship in the room.

The Farchakhs we will see again, rather often, I hope. Afterward, as we stood with our *propriétaires* outside on the landing, Madame Demeulenaere looked a bit wistfully at the door across the hall.

"It seems strange," she said, "to be leaving Georges and

Salma and not just to go in there." Then we went the three steps home, and unlocked our door. And the elevator carried them down and away.

30

THE ROYAL HABIT must be hard to break. For those of us whose national experience has not included resident kings, queens, consorts and all the foppery and extravagance of palace life, the charm of it is hard to understand. But here in Europe, even where officially unfashionable, the latent monarchical tendency remains very strong.

For example, the French, as you probably have heard, had a revolution once. Their rising was not against a foreign colonial power, as ours was, but against their own rulers, and it was a vindictive and sanguinary affair. The well-bred were led to the public square in great numbers and invited to help explore a tantalizing logical and biomechanical question whose answer, in spite of their unselfish contribution, remains unknown to this day: To wit, whether the severed head does or does not hear the cheers of the mob as it falls into the basket.

The stately houses were pillaged and sometimes burned. Monuments were dragged down and smashed. Churches were ransacked for treasure—their bells melted into pigs of iron, the edifices themselves commandeered for storage. The effort, insofar as the few years of The Terror permitted, was to reduce France to the cultural and aesthetic equivalent of a Russian potato farm. And upon that foundation of wreckage the first French republic was raised.

Just short of 200 years ago, that's been. Yet to look at France today is to understand that the attraction of the idea of royalty has been transcendent, after all. Not only have the monuments mostly been put back in place, which is all to the good, and the kingly palaces and country houses restored and refurbished at vast public expense. But strapping country boys and plump-cheeked peasant girls, whose forebears may well have been part of the mob, waving hay sickles and baying for the heads to drop, now get themselves up in silk hose and satin bloomers and powdered wigs and, taking the parts of the vanished nobility, strut and mince through effete dances on the marble courtyards of the châteaux.

You can say that this is only for the benefit of the tourists, for the revenue it brings. And to some extent, of course, that's true. But that does not explain the reverence that transforms the voice of the guide as she ushers yet another clutch of visitors into some royal parlor, some queenly bedchamber—her eyes, her words, her whole manner caressing with unctuous longing the gilded artifacts of a vanished way of life.

Nor does it account for the day-to-day French fascination with the affairs of surviving monarchies elsewhere in this small corner of the world, whose representatives provide a running spectacle of antic conduct that is surpassed, for pure amusement, only by the shenanigans of a few African dictators and some of the uncountable progeny of the House of Saud.

Being in the main powerless and kept as national pets, their problems seem to stem from idleness and boredom. They drive their Maseratis too fast on lanes built for donkey carts. Or they are photographed at seaside resorts with nymphets of lurid reputation, and thus scandalize the royal household. Nothing momentous. And yet these peccadillos command absolutely unrelenting public attention. So that the run of a week's news is like nothing you have ever read before.

Here, for example, is an account of how Prince Albert of Liege, heir to the Belgian throne, fell off his motorcycle north of Fréjus, France, cracking several ribs and skinning his hide on the pavement. Accompanied by someone named Prince Paola, the article says, Prince Albert was vacationing briefly on the Côte d'Azur, after previously vacationing in Sardinia.

Or another item: It seems that the boyfriend of Princess Stephanie of Monaco tried to pass through a border post in a fog at 85 miles an hour in his Mercedes-Benz, crashing into a cement blockade, flattening a traffic sign, demolishing an empty police van and then ramming a parked car. A heavy night's work for any 19-year-old, but he walked away with scratches.

Or here, sadder still: While hunting moor hens on the estate of the Earl of Strathmore in the north of England, one of the titled guests slipped as he was taking aim and bagged, instead of a hen, one of the other hunters and the earl's gamekeeper. Nasty business, that! Bad show! Presumably they picked out the pellets and carried on stiff-lipped.

One gets the impression, following all this in the French papers, that royal blood must carry with it, besides a tendency to hemophilia and madness, a proneness to accidents. It's a pity, really, to have gone to the trouble of a revolution when, given patience and modern technology, the monarchy might simply have vanished at its play.

31

JUST DOWN OUR STREET, at the corner of the third block, a tall wrought-iron gate, unlocked from daylight to dusk, opens through a fence into a square of greenery all but hidden behind its dense periphery of shrubs. Enter, and you find yourself in one of the many vest-pocket *jardins* which, tucked away in surprising places, give escape from the noise and numbers of the pressing city.

This one is called Square Léon Blum. It occupies a single block, bounded in every direction by busy avenues and shops and apartment buildings of various ages. But all that is forgotten when you are inside.

In a corner of the enclosure there is a nursery school and small playground, from which can be heard a happy chirrup of toddlers' voices. The rest is grass and flowers and gravel paths winding under the shade of old trees. At one side, behind a bed of roses, a marble satyr tries to warm the heart of a marble maiden with music from his reed pipes. In the center there is an ornamental pool where two statuary nymphs cavort on a pedestal. The pool is home also to a pair of ducks, who come out to hunt insects in the grass.

Magically, the barrier of foliage mutes the racket of the nearby streets to a murmur as soft as the hum of distant bees. A wooden bench along one of the paths is a fine place to sit and watch an hour or a season pass. Or even, if one must, to work. Before discovering his square, I knew nothing at all about Léon Blum—had never, so far as I can remember, heard his name. But the pleasure I've gotten from that little park prompted me to look him up in a book. Though a minor figure in the whole of French history, evidently he was a formidable man. The photograph shows him at a desk, cravatted, bespectacled and prim, even severe. But pictures can mislead. As a young man in the late 1800s it seems he had a literary bent, wrote poetry and essays and criticism. Then, for the balance of his life, politics engaged him.

In 1936, as leader of a coalition of parties of the French left, he became—in his middle 60s—his country's first Socialist premier. The German wave was gathering to break again over Europe and the world. The Holocaust was shaping in Hitler's mind. And Blum, moreover, was a Jew. Only 13 months he had as France's leader, before his government was turned out of power. But in that short time there were enacted many of the articles of social legislation that still shape and soften the lives of French working people today, including the laws on collective bargaining, the 40-hour work week and mandatory annual paid vacations. It is this he is principally remembered for.

Three years later, after the Nazi occupation of France, Léon Blum was arrested, tried by the Vichy government, sent away in his 70s to a German concentration camp and finally, in 1945, liberated by American soldiers. He died in 1950. Probably I could learn more about him by talking to the elderly widow lady whose door is the third one on our apartment landing. Her husband, I am told, was once the conductor of the Monte Carlo Symphony and was a friend of Blum's. But the truth is that, not being French, it's less his career I care about than just this little park that bears his name along our street.

I have sat there many fine afternoons with my notebook open, sometimes writing in it, more often just listening to the children's voices. And watching *au pairs* of the neighborhood roll babies past in carriages, or old French ladies of the generation before mine as they come limping along the shaded walks, their canes crunching on the gravel, to sit a while themselves and see if this day, possibly, the maiden will answer the satyr's flute. I like to imagine the times through which they have lived.

My favorite bench is the one beside a ceramic pillar, spreading at its top to become the torso and head of a figure convulsed with mirth. Fat bunches of grapes wreathe the face and spill between the fingers that clutch the head in an agony of merriment.

One below the other on the ceramic pillar appear the names of Rabelais, Molière, Voltaire and other French writers long dead, and at the bottom are inscribed the words: *Laughter Is the Right of Man.* Léon Blum, whose laws gave his countrymen more time for laughter, surely would approve of that.

32

I HAVE MET THE MAN with the bad news. After years of getting the bad news secondhand, yesterday it finally happened: I met the man who *has* it. I had come out of a bookstore near the Concorde and crossed a narrow street, dodging a green Citroen that tried to deliver me the bad news ahead of time, when I saw, just ahead, a man with a folding table set up on the sidewalk. Leaning against one leg of the table was a hand-lettered sign that said, in French,

BETTER A PERSHING MISSILE
IN YOUR JARDIN
THAN A RUSSIAN SOLDIER
ON YOUR WIFE.

The streets of Paris are full of people selling everything imaginable. It wasn't clear what this guy was selling, but it was obvious he was hoping for passers-by to talk to. So, passing by, I stopped for a moment.

"Hi," the man said.

"What are you selling?" I asked him.

"I *thought* you were American. What am I selling? I'm selling a strong defense. I don't suppose you're the founder of some peace group?" He said that with a verbal sneer. I ignored the question.

"How do you happen to be selling defense? On a Paris street?"

"Because," he said. "I was involved in the development of *that*." He nodded toward the other side of the walk, where he had set up a big, brightly-illustrated poster of the proposed U.S. "Star Wars" anti-missile system. I looked at the poster and then back at him. He was a handsome fellow, with black hair slicked back, wearing a coat and trousers that almost matched. But his eyes were funny. They were gray—absolutely calm and untroubled. The way the eyes are of people who have received ultimate revelations and gone nutty as fruit cakes.

"Will it work?" I asked him.

"Do you have any background in science?" he asked me back.

"No, but I read the papers. There seems to be some question whether it will work."

"Do you know what this is?" He pointed to one of the books spread out in a display on his table. Its cover, as of most of the others, was a picture of some complicated machine. I didn't know what it was, but it looked a little bit like the kettle my Aunt Julia used to boil Mason jars in.

"What would you say," he asked, "if I told you that temperatures could be contained in that machine which duplicate the inner processes of the sun? Temperatures of millions of degrees." He said it the way the astronomer Carl Sagan does on television, drawing out the first letter: *Mmmmmmmillions*. Come to think of it, he looked a little bit like Carl Sagan.

"I thought you could only do that in a plasma bottle," I said. I was bluffing, but he eyed me with new respect.

"That's what that is. A plasma bottle. Those things around the outside are magnets to hold the energy inside the dough-nut."

I nodded.

"Of course," he said, "that's an order of magnitude less difficult than what we're trying to do here—" He indicated the "Star Wars" poster again. "But it shows what we're capable of."

"Who's 'We'?"

"I'm working for *So-and-so*," he said, pronouncing the name importantly, as if it were someone I should have heard of. But I hadn't. And, as you can see, I have forgotten it again already.

"Who's *So-and-so*?" I asked.

He seemed thunderstruck. He pointed to a paperback book

on the table, with a man's face and the name of *So-and-so* on the cover. It was an ordinary looking face, really a little dopey.

"He's been on prime-time TV at least nine times for as much as a half-hour. He's the man responsible for this system we're talking about. And you've never heard of him? I'm amazed."

"Is he a scientist?"

"Well, in a way, yes."

"I don't see what this has to do with Pershings and Russian soldiers."

"What would you say," he asked, "if I told you the next five months probably are the most dangerous in the whole history of the world?"

"No kidding," I said.

"It will be at least that long before President Reagan can overcome the Russian edge in nuclear weapons. And they also have a slight lead in *that* technology—" He pointed again to the poster. "The Russians see it as their little window of opportunity. And if you put this in the context of the collapse of the world monetary system, which is happening right now, these next five months are very, *verrrrry* dangerous."

His calm eyes searched for the terror in my face.

"What would you say," he said, "if I told you that I wouldn't be surprised if the Russians launched a conventional attack on West Germany at 4 o'clock this afternoon?"

I looked at my watch. "It's already a quarter till 6," I told him. "I'd say we probably would have heard by now."

"Wise guy," he said sadly, and turned away to rearrange his books.

33

THE SCHOOL IS LIKE no other they have attended, or ever may attend again. They will learn the usual things there, I suppose—the manipulation of numbers, the dates of conquests, the inadmissibility of dangling participles. But the first lesson, which I hope they will remember longest, has been how diverse, how fabulously and richly *unalike,* are the peoples with whom they are privileged and doomed to share the planet.

Almost any child of a certain age and normal wit can master geometry. Grammar, literature, atomic weights, the digestive processes of earthworms—all are teachable, and some even worth knowing. Rote learning is not the problem.

The problem of education, particularly for American children, is that too often it takes place among other young people whose view of the world, whose assumptions and expectations and whole cultural experience, with slight variations, are indistinguishable from their own. I did my learning in such a setting, and I remember it as monochromatic. Except in the most superficial ways—physical stature, curl of hair, number of pimples and so forth—my classmates and I were virtual carbon copies of one another. I suspect that if we had gone to the wrong houses at supper time and taken our places at the table, it might have been minutes before our own parents noticed the difference.

Not so in this school. Among my daughters' fellow learners are children of more than 50 nationalities, some of them nearly as baffled by the English language as my daughters are by French. The circumstances that have brought them together here must be many. Company transfers, or some watershed change in a parent's career; the abandonment of a homeland torn by war, broken by tyranny, bled hopeless by corruption. The road to Paris, as to any of the world's great cities, has a thousand beginnings. And those who travel it must have a thousand stories to tell.

A classmate came home with one of our girls the other day. They are working together on an article for the school newspaper, and I pressed upon them my intrusive advice. The classmate's father works for an international firm. This year she will spend in France. Next year her family will go to Indonesia and she will continue her studies in Jakarta or at a boarding school in Singapore. Hers is just one of those stories.

So far, the information carried home to us has been very lean. Usually the school day was "great." Sometimes it was "okay." That's the sum of their report, after which they disappear into their room to begin homework or write letters or do the day's entry in their journals. I would give a lot to read those journal passages, but of course I never will—unless maybe sometime when they are quite grown up and I am old and the memory of this time here together has long gone cold.

The homesickness they must sometimes feel, their anxiety at this new beginning in a place so strange and different, their fascination with those classmates from lands they have only read about in books, their sense of the adventure that opens now before them—all that we're left to guess at, or imagine.

But this much I know. By leaving their own country and friends and all that used to be familiar and comfortable, they have stepped into the world. And it is a journey without final destination, or any road all the way back.

In the early light they go down on the elevator and out. By leaning from the window farther than is sensible to do, I can just see the stop where they wait for the public bus—can see them standing there, sweatered against the cool of morning. "Know the luck of it!" I want to shout out to them. "Miss nothing! Be open to it all!"

But it would sound like frantic gibberish. And anyway the distance is too great. Then the bus comes to block the view.

And they are gone away to where we can only follow in our hopes.

34

THE CROWDS HAVE thinned at the Louvre and the other main attractions. Most of the foreign tourists have gone home, and the ones remaining seem somehow sad and disoriented, like birds left behind by the great migration. Their talk is principally of toilets and of the mail.

In the hot fever of the tourist summer, when travelers are wrapped in the comforting jostle of so many others exactly like themselves, the small oddities and hardships of a strange land can be taken in stride as part of a shared adventure. But that changes in September. September is no time to wander in great need into some Paris brasserie or street café and make one's first acquaintance with the raised tile footprints and crusted orifice of what passes for a *rest* room. See one of those in the wrong season, at an impressionable moment, with the days shortening and the autumn about to turn, and your mind may never have any rest again.

"But, daddy," I heard a child complain the other day, "there *isn't* any toilet."

"Yes there is," the father told him. "The sign says so."

"There isn't though. *There's just . . . there's just . . .*"

"That's the toilet."

Another afternoon I came out of a restaurant and found a woman standing agitated on the sidewalk, turning first one way and then the other, dizzy as a rudderless ship. Then her eyes locked on mine in desperation.

"Did you see a man in the men's room?" she demanded to

know in English.

"Plusieurs, madame," I replied, as coolly as any native. *Several of them.* And left her to wonder if he had perhaps died in there. Or if this time he had left her for good. And whether he had the travelers' checks or whether they were back at the hotel.

Saddest of all are the travelers who wait in the line at the central post office, passports in hand, hoping that among the sheaves of held letters filed alphabetically in boxes—new letters, old letters, last year's letters, dead letters—will be found an envelope that bears their name.

I would like to be able to tell you how many pieces of mail the Paris postal service handles in a day, but I can't. I have been dialing all the listed numbers, and evidently the volume is so great that no one there has time even to answer the telephone. But suffice that the letters must number way into the millions. That anyone would give as a mailing address, *General Delivery, Paris, France,* strikes me as incredible. That anyone else would waste the time to put words on paper and dispatch them to that address is more amazing still. But there is a lot of dim-wittedness in the world. And evidently people do it, because every day the line forms at that window, which is next to the one where I go to post my weekly airmail packets.

The passport is handed to the clerk, who disappears to rummage through the dusty bundles of Cs and Rs and Ws. Often there is some misunderstanding.

"Nothing for Adam," the clerk says wearily.

"My name isn't Adam. My name is—"

"But it says Adam, this passport."

There is grumbling from rearward in the line.

"That's my first name. My last name is Norris. Try under Norris, will you?"

"Well, there is nothing for Morris, either."

"It's Norris. With an N."

"Nothing," says the clerk. And, putting the heavy rubber

band around the sheaf of Ms, shoves the passport back. The supplicant stumbles away empty-handed.

They have a disheveled, strung-out look, the people in that line—the look of people who have overspent their time or their money or both, and who urgently need whatever that envelope is bringing, like a note in a bottle, to *General Delivery, Paris.*

"But there has to be mail," I heard a man say yesterday. "I know there's mail." He refused to accept his passport from the clerk. "You've got to look again."

The man was an Australian. His wife and two children were with him, and they all had that appearance of people too long adrift.

"There must be a letter," he said. "Some people have write me six weeks before now. They say that they have writed me—" He was struggling with the verb forms. Then he remembered it was his native English he was speaking, and he turned to his wife in alarm.

"My God," he cried. "I've forgotten how to talk!"

If late September finds you standing at the held mail window at the Paris post office, you have stayed too long.

35

IT IS TOLD THAT every street in this city, from the magnificent Champs-Élysées to the humblest winding *rue,* is swept every day. That seems to me a somewhat fabulous claim, and how one would set about verifying it I can't begin to say. But on our street, at least, it is true.

Each morning just after dawn—which comes later now, as the weeks march on—a *scritch-scritching* can be heard from below our window, where a man in a blue uniform and cap, with a wheeled hand-cart and a broom of bundled twigs, is passing slowly along the avenue.

First he sweeps clean the space between sidewalk and curb. If the morning is a wet one with the gutters running full, he uses his twig broom to nudge his gatherings into the flood and hasten them on their way to the sewer. On dry days, he loads the litter into his cart.

He goes about his duty in a deliberate, unhurried way—the manner of a man who knows that the street is long and the whole day is ahead of him.

Two nights ago the weather made a marked change. Clouds boiled up behind the hill to the west and, just at dark, came rushing in to set the treetops wildly tossing and fling a torrent of cold rain against the glass. The sharp edge of that wind was, suddenly, no longer just the coolness of an unseasonable summer, but the serious announcement of something finished, something else coming. And there have been other signs. The leaves of the plane trees that border the street have begun ever so slightly to curl and pale, and the ones of the great chestnuts that tower across the way have taken on a faint russet look as they dry and redden at their outer edges.

Sitting yesterday at a table of the café on our circle, bundled in sweaters like all the other loiterers, we noticed how the birches planted in the circle's center trembled and glittered in the breeze like trees of silver coins. On close inspection, the foliage of the birches hadn't changed at all. It must have been the different angle of the light.

We have not seen a single squirrel in the city. There may be some here, somewhere. But we haven't come across them. There are only pigeons, feckless mendicants. And unlike squirrels they are without forebodings, are seized by no frenzy of autumn thrift. They just sit stupidly on the lamp posts and chimney pots, planing up against the pale sky for the useless joy of it, then coming back to perch, taking change as it comes.

The last of the local vegetables are disappearing from the stores. The berries are long finished, and the apricots brought up from the coast are green and hard.

The apartment cat in the facing building still comes out in the morning onto his 10th-floor ledge, but enjoys it less, or at least does not stay as long. Windows are kept mostly closed, so that in the afternoons tantalizing smells are no longer wafted in to us from Salma Farchakh's kitchen, which is next to ours.

And the waiter, Serge, who has brought us nearly all our summer coffees, told us yesterday that he is leaving the café on our circle—going to take a better job at a real restaurant on the Avenue de la Grande Armée just down from the Arc de Triomphe. Nothing stays the same.

This morning, for the first time since our coming, I got out of bed in darkness. And even after dressing and making coffee, it is only just now light. The room is cold. But from the street below I can hear, even through the closed glass, the *scritch-scritch* of the twig broom of the man who cleans our street. In the season past he swept dropped papers and burnt cigarette ends and broken pieces of bottles.

This morning he is sweeping leaves.

Season's end

In Changing Light

36

CHARTRES . . . LE MANS. Worthy destinations in themselves, but now only names to mark the miles on a night road bearing southwest across half the breadth of France toward the coast and the great waterfowling marsh of Brittany, *La Grande Brière*. And at 9 o'clock in the parking lot of the train station at Saint-Nazaire the guide, Bernard Deniaud, is waiting. With him, we cross the street to a brasserie for late supper of coffee and a sandwich.

"Not many ducks," Bernard says. The sandwich is half a fat loaf, with a rumor of ham concealed somewhere in its mass. "Usually in October there are many." Two weeks before, a gale blew in with driving rain. Bernard's brother went out on the marsh and expended 43 *cartouches,* nearly two boxes of shells, in an hour, bringing home 11 ducks.

"But now, as you can see," he says, "the weather is too fair. No coldness. No tempests from the sea. The great flights do not come down yet from Holland and the north countries. Some ducks, yes. But they are few."

With me is my hunting friend from home, Patrick Dolan. In his experience and mine, *few*ness is the natural condition of ducks. He is a good hunter, Dolan, and more important he is a lucky one. If he enters the woods in November and stands beside a tree, antlered deer walk by. In the spring, wild turkey gobblers fall over one another to be the first into his roaster. Ducks are a different matter. They figure large in our autumn mythology. We listen, only half-believing, to other hunters' tales of huge success. But when we go for ducks ourselves—which has been fairly often—what we see are azure skies traversed by herons, the odd cormorant or two and occasional stupendous flights of crows. Why should it be any different on a French marsh than on a Middle Western pond?

Undismayed by Bernard's report of few ducks—indeed, reassured by the normalcy of it—we follow him out of Saint-Nazaire, his taillights disappearing at the bends of the narrow road, toward the country lodging he has arranged for us near the hunting grounds. Rooms are not easily found this time of year. Prosperity has passed the Bretons by. Their tourist season is slight and short, and when it ends, the auberges, or country inns, shutter their upper windows, though meals may still be gotten.

Bernard Deniaud turns off the paved road onto a gravel lane. The lane branches and becomes a trail, a tunnel through the overhanging boughs of trees. The cars stop before a house, of which little can be seen except the lighted entry. A small, neat woman appears on the step. And around the outer corner of the place, out of darkness, a gaunt man comes striding. We present ourselves to them. People in their 40s, I'd guess them to be—although work and disappointment give them an older look. There in the deep of their forest, they wait for roomers.

"At 5 o'clock, then," Bernard says. "Come to my house and we will take breakfast—coffee and some brioches." On the road out from town he has shown us where he lives, not five minutes from the marsh. Hands are shaken all around, and Deniaud's car vanishes back into the tunnel of the trees. We will need to rise at 4 a.m., but we have no clock. The woman takes a watch from her wrist and sets its alarm. "It will sound five times," she warns. "Ding-ding. Then it will stop. It is automatic."

The house, inside, is immense—cavernous and chilly, with midnight nearing. We are on the third floor in a large, two-bedded room, clean and comfortably appointed, with

100

heavy comforters atop the blankets and plumbing across the hall. Footsteps sound a short while on the wooden floors below. Then there is only the wrapping stillness of the forest that presses close.

And, immediately it seems, the borrowed watch strikes its five small chimes to declare an end of sleeping.

Breakfast in the kitchen of a country man: buns, with jam and farm butter from a pot; coffee served in a bowl, the bowl warming cupped hands as it is raised to drink. The morning is not cold, but men still tremble at that hour, as dogs do, waiting for the hunt.

Down a short lane, then, to the mooring and Deniaud's boat, hand-made of wood, flat-bottomed and narrow at the stern, six meters long, a bit over 19 feet. Guns are put in, and the canvas bag of Bernard's *formes,* 10 molded decoys. Then the five live mallards, four hens and a drake, silent in their wooden box. Then finally the motor gas. He will use the outboard on the east-west main canal that traverses the marsh. But once near the blind, he will lift the motor and maneuver deftly with the slender pole that was, for generations, the Brière boatman's sole propulsion.

Cyrus, Deniaud's Labrador retriever, has been prospecting at the marsh's edge. At a call he comes heavy-footed out of the darkness and settles in the boat beside the box of captive ducks. The plank seats are dew-wet. With two practiced thrusts of the pole, the boat is backed into the canal and turned. The motor is started.

One could hunt all of a lifetime and much of the next without the eye recording a more memorable picture. Bernard, wild-haired, wild-bearded Breton marshman, standing in the back to watch for hummocks in the channel as he steers, a dark figure against the slightly-less-dark sky, the full moon a hand's breadth above his right shoulder, the wake curling away like polished pewter in the moonlight, the fine head of the retriever profiled against the shine of water. And ahead, torn mist trails curling among the reeds, the still surface of the canal cut in Vs by water creatures hurrying to their dens.

A quarter-hour, we've come. Then, where the channel widens, he kills the motor, puts out his *formes* and after those his live ducks, wings pinioned, anchored by cords and weights. Freed from their box, they chuckle and speak to one another. And Bernard poles into the blind, which is exactly boat-shaped, well-concealed with bundles of the reeds that thatch the roofs of many houses of that neighborhood.

When can shooting commence? "There is no time by law," Deniaud says. "Whenever you can see." And if ducks should come, how many may be taken? Of which sex and what variety? *"Illimité,"* he says—no limit.

Across the stillness a church bell rings. Then, from a different quarter, another. Then still another. From the steeples of villages all around the margins of that reedy wilderness, the faithful are being told the hour, which is 6 o'clock and still full dark. What we're likeliest to see, says Bernard, is the *col-vert,* or green-neck, which we call a mallard. But teal also use the marsh. And shovelers and red-heads. And a duck that, seen by flashlight in the book he carries, appears to be a variety of scaup. The mallards will rest the winter here, where the ice rarely is more than a skim among the reeds. The others go on—to the Mediterranean and beyond, to North Africa.

Waiting for light, we have heard from the marsh around us a chorus of plaintive cries. They are made, Bernard says, by the creatures we saw swimming ahead of the boat. Three names he calls them by: *ragondin* and *miocastor* and, commonly, just *rat.* Some relative of the muskrat, but larger by three times at least, they were brought years ago from South America to be bred for their pelts. Then some escaped into the wild. For a while men trapped them, until their incredible multiplication broke the market.

The sky pales. Several high flights of mallards pass over far out of range. *Briérons* do not use artificial calls, depending on their decoys to do the hailing. But Bernard's ducks, so talkative in the dark, now ignore these occasional appearances of their kin. Between times, Deniaud speaks of the marsh itself.

Nearly 17,000 acres in extent, it was formed many thousand years ago when alluvial deposits from the Loire, just to the south, and the Vilaine River to the north cut off the basin from the sea and drowned the ancient forests. Since the 16th century, when it was given to them in perpetuity by Queen Anne of Brittany, the Brière has belonged to the people whose houses and villages abut its shores—who have dug peat from it, fished, hunted, trapped eels and grazed their sheep and cattle among its rushes in the dry season.

The sun is full risen now over the watery domain of which Deniaud, his wife, Claudette, and their 12-year-old daughter, Eva, are part-owners. Not of any parcel of it, but of it all, in common with some 50,000 other *Briérons*.

The marsh, he says, has changed little in his lifetime. His father once caught a pike of 10 kilos—22 pounds. Now the fish are mostly small. The greatest change has been the gasoline motor. With only a pole to push the boat, it used to take four hours to reach the hunting place. Bernard remembers when he and his brother, both still too small to shoot, would go with their father and sleep the night in the bottom of the boat. And the next day they would bring back sacks of ducks.

"Sacks of them!" he says, amazed at the memory.

Suddenly, as he talks, a mallard pair comes quartering in, high and fast. Three shots, three misses. The ducks fly on. For this hunt, no sacks will be needed. The retriever, Cyrus, looks disappointed. From some distance across the marsh, the hum of an outboard engine is heard.

Bernard Deniaud and Cyrus

"Fishermen," Deniaud says. "Or maybe reed-cutters." He looks at the empty sky. "For the morning it is finished. Tonight we will try a different way."

On a lane where few travelers are seen, the Auberge Haut Marland waits with its dozen tables prettily set. And at the ebb of the season, it is glad even for hunters in their rough attire.

Half an avocado, ripe to perfection, is filled with crabmeat. After that there is a huge bowl of mussels, only three miles and a few hours from the sea, steamed in their spicy broth. And after that a duck glazed golden in the roasting. And a bottle of Bordeaux to wash all that down. Whatever happens in the marsh in the morning, you are assured of your limit in the Haut Marland at noon.

We drive back along the road, turn off through the tunnel of trees. And while Dolan rests from all that exercise at table, I make the acquaintance of our hosts, who are François de la Monneraye and his wife, Cécile. And who, I learn, are the proprietors of a considerable estate.

The 500-acre forest, the 16th-century manor house and barns, the later house—the château, he calls it—in which we slept, have been in the family for 450 years. But keeping it is the problem. Every year, they say, the taxes are worse. The orangerie has fallen into ruin. The chapel became first a gardener's hut and then, when the gardener left, a leaky storage shed. Beetles have killed the forest's elms, though its oaks and cedars are safe.

Monsieur de la Monneraye still has two guns. But he has given up the chase, being obliged instead to sell the rights to hunt the hares and pigeons and the boars and roebucks he claims still are often seen. To heat the château and manor house, he has erected under a lean-to midway between them a gigantic wood-fired boiler, operating on a system of valves and pumps.

The thing burns *33 cords of wood a year.*

"But you see," he cries with crazy defiance, waving at the forest all around, "I have much wood!"

Everywhere there is a sense of relentless crumbling and decay which Madame de la Monneraye's brave beds of marigolds can little slow, much less prevent. In the manor house—the end of it in best repair—they have made an apartment to rent. And on the upper floor of the château they take paying guests for the night. But even in season, the travelers they get are of a threadbare class—noisy, they say, and not always clean.

"Once we had a family of Norwegians," says the madame. "And they were very, very nice." The lord of the manor nods his agreement. "But the others—well, the others are not always so proper." And again he nods, with the sadness of someone who must know that propriety has escaped him for good.

The rest is quickly told.

Deep twilight finds us standing in the marsh in wading boots, facing the direction from which Bernard thinks the ducks might come. It will be just at dark, and it is tricky shooting, he warns.

"You hear the wings. You turn. You shoot."

Through the fringe of head-high reeds the lights of Saint-Nazaire can be seen to the southeast. The moon is not quite risen. The footing is uncertain and the whole enterprise seems futile and dangerous. I pray that no ducks come. The prayer is answered.

Afterward there is supper at Bernard's house, with a fire burning on the open hearth. He pours glasses of Pernod, which I am told has been the ruin of many Breton men, although his taste for it seems to be moderate. He and his wife ask about Paris. She believes it must be miserable, though she has never been there and has no desire to go. "For me," she says, "Paris is *un autre monde"*—another world.

The second morning's sky is as cloudless as the first, and even emptier of ducks. Poling across a long shallow to a different blind, we hear the mutter and rustle of ducks sleeping on the flats. But when day comes they are gone. The two electric moments are when Bernard's decoys announce, with excited quacking, the appearance of a vagrant songbird and later of an airplane overhead.

The sun bears down stiflingly. Midges circle our faces. We listen to the church bells chime away the morning, and to the small, sad cries of the *rat*.

"Pas de canards," Bernard says finally. No ducks. And searching our faces for disappointment, finds none at all. It is amusing to hear other hunters' stories about ducks. It is nice to imagine mornings of sacks of them. But to actually get them would be, in the end, only a perishable pleasure. It doesn't matter, we reassure him. There never are any ducks.

37

THE UPSTAIRS PIANO PLAYER is back. After nearly six weeks of unexplained silence, the music has resumed in the apartment overhead. The first note was struck yesterday morning, and since then, with time out only for sleep, the playing has been continuous.

Beginning on the day we took this flat, and for weeks afterward, the music from up above was the accompaniment of all our waking hours. From the instant of rising until 10 o'clock at night, excepting meal times, we were treated to a most amazing display of skill and raw endurance. In the course of the day's long march there were inevitable digressions, but nearly all of that energy seemed to be poured into the mastery of a single classical piece. Majestically full-chorded, almost martial, the playing of it was. And while we might have preferred a bit more variety, I can say honestly that we received many hundred hours of pleasure from listening to that one composition. Or maybe it was many thousands hours. Anyway, a lot.

And who was this upstairs virtuoso? We decided it must be a woman in her middle years—alone most likely, having suffered some wound of the heart or reverse in her career, or both, but remembering what might have been and dreaming still of one last triumph on the concert stage.

No sooner had we puzzled that out than the music stopped. Just stopped completely. Not one tentative note was heard; not one scrape of the piano bench on the floor that is our ceiling. The first still day passed into the next, and the days into silent weeks.

One adjusts to change. But, even so, at odd moments we would catch ourselves wondering, with a vague unease, what it might be that had quieted those nimble hands. And for how long? Then yesterday we were glad to learn that we had worried needlessly. For, as abruptly as it stopped, the playing commenced again—although, as I've said, with a difference. No longer does the morning begin with a rigorous hour of finger exercises. No longer is the breakfast-to-bedtime recital dominated by the majestic formality of that piece on which so many summer hours were spent. In fact, it hardly is played at all—a few preliminary chords of it, at most, trailing off then into something else distracted and aimless.

Aimless. That's just the word for what we hear from above us now. Aimless and romantic and melancholy. Where once there was discipline and stern purpose, now there is only a saccharine repertoire of sonatas, nocturnes and mushy, romantic tunes of the popular kind.

I don't have to be told what has happened. She took an

end-of-summer trip. Probably it was to the seashore, which can be dangerously affecting at a certain age. She met someone there, and I can imagine it all: the weathered clapboard of the quaint French inn; the table beside a window, looking out through lace curtains to the sparkle of wave and rush of cloud; the sense of lives and seasons changing; the modest wine overpriced.

The inn had a piano. She played for him—the majestic piece. But he, a Perrier salesman from Lyon, wanted something sweeter. So now, all discipline gone out of her, she plays only sentimental things. Against her better judgment, she has taken one more chance in the lottery of life. But there's no happiness for her. She will be hurt yet again.

Then the concert will end forever in the apartment directly overhead. And Madame Freguin, the concierge, will stop receiving unpleasant calls from other tenants, whose walls are no thinner than ours are but whose devotion to the arts must be less.

38

A FRIEND OF A FRIEND called to say he was stopping in town on his way home from Geneva. He was on an expense account and staying in the pricy part of town, so he proposed that we meet at his hotel and walk together over to Harry's New York Bar on the Rue Daunou.

If you think you might come to Paris sometime and are making a list of things to do, Harry's Bar is a good one to leave off your list. The place is a bit too self-consciously *New Yorkish*. The tariff is stiff. The portions are too ample. Time gets away there, and no good can come of it. But that's another story.

Although this new acquaintance pretended he had never been to Harry's before, it seemed significant that he knew a short-cut. Just up the street from the hotel where he was lodged is the back door of the Ritz, which is said by some to be the most famous hotel in the world and also one of the most expensive.

Going in that door off the Rue Cambon, we passed the Hemingway Bar which appeared to be closed—and which is right up there with Harry's on the list of places to miss—then turned down a broad, block-long corridor only slightly less ostentatious than the Hall of Mirrors at Versailles, coming out finally through the front door of the Ritz onto the Place Vendôme. Not once in all that march did I see a chair that looked as if it were actually made to be sat upon. One supposes that the furniture in the more than 200 rooms and suites must be more inviting, since it is hard to imagine even American starlets and Arab sheiks laying out that kind of money to spend the night standing up in a shower stall.

But neither were we molested on our way. Whether it was plain luck, or whether my acquaintance somehow just had the manner for it, our right to walk in one door of the Ritz and out the other was not challenged.

So I filed that away in my mind, with other random information. And yesterday, when I happened again to be crossing the Place Vendôme and got caught in a sudden, nasty spit of rain, I thought to myself, *Well, like any old Paris hand, I will simply step into the front door of the Ritz here. And by the time I come out the other side, maybe the rain will have stopped. Or, great as the distance is, maybe I will have passed into a different climatic zone.*

So I proceeded inside, and had taken about three steps along the Hall of Mirrors when an enormous tuxedoed figure loomed in my path. Impeccable tailoring gave to this figure a false impression of slimness. When in fact, based on the space it filled and the amount of light it blocked, its sheer bulk had to be considerable.

"*Habitez-vous ici?*" it inquired. *You live here?*

It smiled. That is, it bent over me, like Tyrannosaurus Rex, and showed its teeth.

"No," I told it. "I'm just—heh, heh—passing through to the Rue Cambon."

The figure raised its eyebrows in disbelief. Then wagged from side to side, in mute reproof, a bejeweled pinky finger the size of a sausage. I made my craven retreat back out into the rain.

So much for short-cuts through the Ritz. But I have been inside it once. And, like Harry's Bar, once is enough. I do not plan to go back there again unless I own the place. Last night I fantasized how it might go. I will come in off the Place Vendôme as I did yesterday, wearing my usual slightly scuffed and seedy look, and the big toothy one lurking in the Hall of Mirrors will step out to block my way.

"Do you live here?" it will demand to know.

"No, my little monsieur"—for that's what I will call him. "I don't live here. *I own the joint.*"

"But that's not possible. The Egyptians own it."

"Until 20 minutes ago they did. I just bought it. Believe me, it's possible. You may collect your check at the window. And now, my little monsieur, if you'll excuse me . . ."

And as the air goes out of him, as out of an inflatable toy, I will stride past him and straight on through and out of there to the Rue Cambon, where I will book a room in some hotel with chairs fit to sit in.

39

THE TYPEWRITER BREAKS every week now. It is an old machine and, as one of the various repairmen said, *très fatiguée*. It is very tired.

These collapses used to signal a major crisis. I would give a howl of dismay, gather up the parts and strike off into the maze of the city in blind hope of finding someone who could fix the thing and enable me to continue with my life. Sometimes I was lucky. More often the shop was closed, or had relocated in some far district on a street not shown on maps. I would come home at noon, a picture of beaten futility, still carrying the typewriter, take nourishment, rest an hour and stumble out again.

But now I have found the place where typewriters like mine are *made*. The factory is in an industrial park nearly two hours distant, first by métro and then by bus. But if I leave at daybreak they will repair it there immediately, while I take coffee and a croissant at a café nearby, and I can be home and working again by noon. So it is an inconvenience, nothing worse. The terror is gone; the typewriter is immortal.

Such small discoveries are one means by which you come finally to be comfortable in a place. But there are other and more personal ways. At first, every face that looks back at you is a stranger's face. Then, to some of those, histories attach. There are recognitions when you pass.

For instance, Monsieur Leclerc, the butcher whose shop is a block down the street and around the corner, can be found every morning in Le Clap's bar. Passing there, you will see him round and pink-faced, exactly as a French butcher ought to look, beginning his day with a copy of *Le Figaro* and a drink of some clear, oily fluid in a glass. He ends each day at Le Narval, the brasserie on the corner, with a glass, or several, of something of a darker color. How much of what he has in between I can't say. But by the time he has drawn his shade and gotten over to Le Narval he is overcome with jolliness.

He likes to press up close, his face directly in yours, and tell about the trip he once made to California, Las Vegas, Miami and Acapulco. "*Très cher, Acapulco!*" he says. Very expensive! And he shakes his hand as if it had been burned. He will tell it every evening if you let him. "This American," he declares loudly, as I am backing off, trying to put a step between us, "has a dog like mine." All the faces turn. "Would you believe it? Just like mine." I once made the mistake of mentioning that to Monsieur Leclerc about his Brittany spaniel, which sits all day just inside the door of his shop. Now he delivers his announcement whenever the two of us are present.

So that's what mostly is known of me: I am American, and I have a dog like the butcher's. It's not a lot, but it's a start.

Jean-Pierre, the husband of Madame Freguin, went to the préfecture of police the other day to speak about the rash of robberies in our building. He received little satisfaction and, what's more, he slipped on the stair coming out and broke his leg. He hobbles about now on crutches, the leg in a cast. And Madame Freguin is obliged to drag out the *poubelles*, which are the building's trash containers, to the curb.

The building is a big one. A couple of hundred people make a lot of trash. When I happen to be going in or out, and see her struggling with the bags, I carry them out to the street for her. Probably she will mention that to someone. And then, besides having a dog like the butcher's, I will also be known as the man who hauls Madame Freguin's *poubelles* while her husband is disabled. My reputation will grow.

With the departure of our waiter, Serge, we have abandoned the café on the circle, whose owner is taciturn and slow. And have taken our business—which is not inconsiderable, amounting to 17 francs each day for one coffee-*crème* and a pot of tea—to Le Narval.

Timing our visit to be finished before Monsieur Leclerc can come from his shop to tell yet again about Acapulco and the dog, we sit at a sidewalk table and watch the other regulars arrive, many of them young people dressed for a guerrilla war. If you are in your early 20s in Paris, the style this autumn is to look like you have just come out of the jungles of Nicaragua, your outfit heavy with grenade loops and bandoliers. We are known there. We draw no stares.

The typewriter factory is in a suburb on a high road above Paris to the southwest. Coming back from there today, my machine already fixed and it hardly even past 10 o'clock, I looked at the city spread out below in the sparkling fall football morning. I could spy our bend of the river and, roughly, our neighborhood, into whose workings we have been folded.

What luck! I suddenly thought. *What an easy place to live!*

The sense of unmanageable strangeness finally abates. Not immediately, but it happens. One day you simply notice it is gone—with an abruptness to make the moment worth remembering.

40

WOULD IT SURPRISE YOU to know that even on an afternoon in October, with the sky low and sunless, a light rain falling and leaves spinning slowly down, the cemetery of Montmartre can be a cheerful and inviting place?

From the bridge of Rue Caulaincourt that crosses above it, the cemetery with its jumble of gabled and porticoed miniature stone houses looks like a little village. Seen closer, those are the crypts and reliquary chapels. And nearly all of them are old—some very old. Doric columns have tilted. Iron-grated doors have rusted off their hinges and, inside, urns have fallen and broken into shards.

Sadness, though it must once have had its day there, long ago passed away. There is about it all a kind of tranquil logic. The sleepers had their turns, and used them well or not, and they rest now untroubled by regret or by anybody's grieving.

For another thing, the cemetery is by no means lifeless. You pass along the lanes—tree-shaded and each one named—of that village of stone, and there is a sense of life teeming at every hand. From some dark aperture, a pair of eyes peering. In the lane ahead, something crossing shadow-quick. In the recesses of a collapsing sepulcher, more eyes. Wherever you venture inside those walls, your movements are watched.

How many cats live there? How would anyone possibly know? Very, very many, though—an absolute *enormousness* of cats, declared the woman caretaker met along one of the lanes. Cats of every color and disposition. Ones with litters of kittens tumbling behind. Others solitary. And all of them tended daily, I understood her to say, by someone from the town hall of Montmartre. So, far from being just squatters there, they are fully welcome. Their pans of food and water are set inside the doors of the crypts, out of the rain. Sleek as show animals, wanting nothing, they have found paradise where most go only in the faintest hope of it. And their careless happiness animates the stones.

But the main reason the cemetery is so inviting is the excellence of the company.

Not far inside the entry, the novelist Émile Zola holds forth in polished red granite, the great head craggy and leonine under the arching trunks of what might be granite trees. On down the Avenue de la Crois you come upon Stendhal, his funerary profile as stubborn and didactic as the vast, soporific masterwork he inflicted on all the oppressed scholars of literature who have followed.

Turn right at the Avenue de Montmorency and you pass Alexander Dumas, lying full-length in classic white marble on the vault lid beneath a marble canopy, staring up vainly at his own words written on the canopy's underside. Farther on in that direction, almost at the boundary wall, is a more modest tomb, with its occupant's face in a bronze plaque on the door. Under the wide artist's beret, the features are self-indulgent, a little coarse. He is Edgar Degas, the painter, triumphant over the critics of his day. On the threshold there is a wilted flower and a clown some visitor has made by stacking broken bits of stone.

So many gifted ones are here—the composers Berlioz and Offenbach, other painters and writers, philosophers, actors from the stage. All content now in their accomplishments. It is, in a way, the last, the greatest *salon*.

One can imagine them waiting for dark to come and the gate to be locked, then getting stiffly up to meet among all the cats in a stone house at the corner of a cemetery avenue to take their evening brandy and argue fiercely, as such people would, about the weight of words, the possibilities of color, the vexing, plastic shapes of life.

But that's impossible, you say. *They're all dead.* Then you cross the city to a gallery and stand before the canvases of one of them, and vitality pours from it still with a freshness to smite the eye and heart. Or you take down a book from the shelf and open its cover, and phrases spring off the page with a force perfectly undiminished.

It is true that the occupants of Montmartre cemetery will write no more stories or paint no more pictures. But except in the strictest medical sense, *dead* is a word that poorly describes their condition.

41

THE STANDARD RENTAL CONTRACT obliges a tenant to insure his landlord's interest against theft of the furnishings, fires, explosions and *dégâts des eaux*, or damages of water.

I suppose a thief might take our valuables, if we had any. But on our tiny elevator, two people make a load and more than three are not allowed. So our proprietor's furniture is safe. The mystery is how he ever got it in. Fires, happily, are rare. And explosions are all but unheard of. So for coverage against the first three hazards you might say we are wasting our money. *Dégâts des eaux* are another matter. Given the state of the art of French plumbing, misfortunes with water may be expected as a matter of course.

Early in our occupancy a rather steady rivulet was noticed eddying out from under the refrigerator and collecting in a pool on the tile of the kitchen floor. Conscientious renter that I am, I telephoned the landlord's sister, who is handling his affairs, and told her I thought we had on our hands an incipient *dégât of eau*. She said, however, that the refrigerator had done that since it was new. Unless the torrent enlarged, there was no cause to worry.

Some days later a uniformed inspector came—to verify the pressure of the building, Madame Freguin explained. It may be that the water in the lines is required by published regulation— the French are keen on regulations—to flow at a force of a certain number of pounds. Evidently the inspector was unsatisfied. He made some adjustment. Immediately the pipes in all the walls set up a thunderous clanking. And not many minutes after that the rubber washers in half the faucets burst, so that the taps could not be shut off.

The water gushed out of them at a rate to gladden the heart of any bureaucrat. The bathroom grew thick with steam. But the worst crisis was at the wash basin, which we kept from overflowing only by bailing with a saucepan and emptying the excess into the tub. Then the tub itself began to fill, despite the drain being fully open.

I sent a runner for Madame Freguin, with news that the inspector had done his work too well. She came immediately and together we strained at the most critical faucet—the hot one in the basin—until the stem twisted off and the handle came free in my grasp. At the last possible instant I found a shut-off valve on the wall pipe and the people who live below us were spared a wetting. But since I had broken the faucet, the *robinet* Madame Freguin called it, a plumber would have to be gotten. She would telephone one for me.

After several days, during which we managed to draw water and sparingly clean ourselves by manipulating the wall valve, the plumber in fact appeared—a compact, affable fellow who had a teen-age apprentice with him. What he did not have was any sign of a tool. A broken *robinet*, he assessed our problem to be, which was fairly obvious since the pieces of it lay there in the basin.

Did we have a knitting needle? he inquired. After that he asked for a kitchen knife. While the apprentice leaned against a wall, watching with moderate interest, he poked futilely with those a while inside the broken fitting. Then, needing heavier armament, he sent the lad down five floors for a single wrench. And when that was delivered, sent him down again for a washer.

The repair, in the end, was make-shift. By leaning on the handle a certain way, water can be made to come out. By leaning another way, it can more or less be stopped. But the *robinet* is finished—*mort*, the plumber said. He would have to come back and replace it. We wait for him to do that. It will soon be a month.

The puddle on the kitchen floor we have learned to step

around. Every faucet drips, some more than others, and worse at certain hours. Our bathroom adjoins the water closet of the next apartment, with only a wall between. When I finish bathing and turn the lever to empty the tub, I think I can hear our neighbors' toilet flush. And any day, I expect, it will be time for the inspector to come round again and turn the pressure up.

Fires and explosions I seldom think about. But where the plumbing is concerned, one sleeps better knowing the policy is paid.

42

I HAVE JUST laid aside a newspaper article describing the last decade of economic failure in the Soviet Union, one aspect of which has been that system's inability to adequately feed its own subjects. While reading this, I happened to be eating, first, two flaky rolls stuffed with ham and melted cheese from the shop of Monsieur Billou, the *pâtissier* just down the street, followed by a puffy, cream-filled obscenity topped by delicate green icing and dusted with shaved chocolate.

Soon I may be indistinguishable in physique from any beet-bagger on a Russian collective farm, but I will have gotten there by a better road than vodka and boiled potatoes.

One cannot live several months in France without achieving a clearer understanding of the role of cuisine in the evolution of societies and the eventual destinies of nations. For example, in any discussion of the torpor and instability of much of modern Africa, the *fufu factor* is rarely if ever mentioned.

The daily fare of millions of Africans—virtually the whole populations of some countries—consists of cassava root and yam pounded into a bland goo that is plucked up with the fingers and placed into the mouth with a manner of solemn introspection. This stuff is called *fufu*, and the prospect of eating it for the rest of your natural life would make you solemn, too. So how does an African politician instill in the masses a zeal for the hard labor of national development? By promising them more *fufu*? Forget it! A little *fufu* goes a long way.

The problem faced by the contemporary Czars of Russia is essentially the same. Beetroot soup and boiled potatoes may nourish, but they do not inspire. Today's Russian has traded his independence of mind and voice for a mess of pottage. Now he would like to trade his mess of pottage for an occasional lamb shank or plate of beefsteak. But that isn't in the 5-year plan, and it can't be arranged. As a result, he works neither happily nor very hard. And the Soviet economy slips deeper into the doldrums, meaning leaner rations and even less work.

Setting out the other day on an aimless meander, I found myself in the Les Halles quarter of the city—the area where the great central market of Paris used to stand, before being razed several years ago to make way for redevelopment. Even with Les Halles gone, it remains a district dedicated to food. There you find the Bourse du Commerce, the trading place of the grain, flour, wine and other commodities brokers, and a practical infinitude of restaurants of various sorts.

The narrow street I wandered along, the Rue Montorgueil, is not an important thoroughfare. But the chance to walk it, just once in a lifetime, would be the nearest thing to Heaven on Earth for half the population of the planet. It is a street of food merchants, and all the fabulous richness of agricultural France can be found there.

In the open stalls hang great slick haunches and sides of beef, marbled and shiny-red. Next to those may lie 200 plucked chickens, arranged like nudists on a beach. And slabs of bacon, baskets of pigs' feet, dressed rabbits, crates of brown country eggs so fresh there are feathers still among them. Thrust out

On the Rue Montorgueil

clear to the curb from other stalls are bins of fish and crustaceans only hours from the sea. And tables of mounded produce—vegetables from the environs of the city; fruit trucked up at night from the south; the first of the year's harvest of Muscat grapes, translucent green and as big, nearly, as plums.

For several blocks it continues that way. Between the stalls you find an occasional bakery or confectioner's shop, or a stand-up counter from which floats the smell of spiced things cooking, or a store selling skillets, pots, knives and other implements for the kitchen. Everything there has in some way to do with food. There are stalls that cater to the immigrant trade, and I even saw a man standing hopefully beside a cart piled high with yams and cassava roots. But he was doing no business. Any African who has seen Paris is finished for good with *fufu*. People wander freely in the street, and nearly everyone you see is carrying a basket of food or bending to eat something dripping and delicious, wrapped in paper, bought at an open counter along the way.

I thought of the Rue Montorgueil a few moments ago, as I was eating my pastries and reading about Soviet disappointments. The year's harvest again was small, the paper said. Food stocks on the shelves are lean. But societies are shaped by the choices they make.

There can be little doubt that the French, if they threw their whole resources into it for a generation, to the exclusion of all else, could manufacture almost as many missiles as the Russians have. But they have chosen not to do that. They are content, instead, to be a *culinary superpower*. And the president of France sleeps easier in his bed at night than any Soviet first secretary ever will.

43

A PLEASANT FIVE-BLOCK stroll north from our traffic circle, or one métro stop and a shorter walk if that's preferred, is the forested playground of the Bois de Boulogne. And at this near end of the Bois are the hippodromes of Longchamp and Auteuil, the two most famous horse racing courses of Paris and among the better known in the world.

Yesterday we tried our luck at Longchamp. Now that we have discovered this source of instant wealth, the tone of these notebook entries is apt to change. Instead of cemeteries and the weather and such, you can expect to be reading quite a bit about the quips and bright little pleasantries that we and the Duc and Duchesse of Such-and-Such have been tossing back and forth between our regular tables at Maxim's and La Tour d'Argent.

All Frenchmen plan to be rich. Judging from the crowd waiting in line at the tobacco counter to buy tickets in the national lottery, most of them plan to be rich after next week's drawing, which could be worth a first prize of 2 million francs or more. As for myself, I'm not particular how it happens— whether by numbers being drawn out of a wheel or horses running around the track. It takes a little longer to get rich at the races than it does at Loto, but there is more of a sense of personal involvement and I think I will be prouder of my wealth if it is honestly earned, instead of being gotten by blind chance.

In yesterday's first race I put 20 francs on the nose of a filly named Children's Corner. The betting windows—at least the lower-denomination windows—are too few, the throng in the area around them jostling and unruly. If you wait to go up there until you've seen the horses parade before the race, you will never get your money down. But who could pass up a name like Children's Corner? So I made my investment and went back to my seat.

Then Children's Corner came out with the others. She was all black, and not glossy black—dirty black, like she'd been wallowing in coal dust. She already looked tired. "Well," I told my wife, "Du Pont and Niarchos didn't make theirs in a day." Those two seem to own a lot of the horses that run in France, although, significantly, they didn't own mine.

The races here go clockwise. Because Longchamp is such a long course—nearly two miles around the full outer oval—the usual race is a little more than a half-lap, starting on the far side and ending just left of the grandstand. Children's Corner came out of the gate fast. Then they went behind some trees and vanished into the distance of the far turn. It was a long time before they came in decent view down the stretch.

A black horse seemed to be in front. People were screaming. "Isn't that her?" my wife asked.

Children's Corner paid 16 to 1. And I began to wonder if you needed a tuxedo at Maxim's or if my gray suit would do.

In the second race, Val de Song, sired by an Irish horse named African Song, had a nice sound to it. But Val de Song finished out of the money. In the third, Matin d'Été—Summer Morning—struck me as appealing, except for being ridden by a jockey named Junk. So we scanned the huge field of 16 entries and settled on an American horse, Northern Native. Native came third, while Summer Morning and Junk won going away.

The fourth race was another big field of 13. The smart money was on a horse named Alloy, but that had a phony sound to it so we went with Duke of Silver, the real thing. The horses paraded to the post. "Too small," I told my wife. Alongside all those bigger animals, Duke of Silver looked like a carnival pony. The announcer calling the race didn't mention him once, and when they came off the last turn the Duke was too far back to be seen.

"Throw away the ticket," I told my wife. Then, on the outside of the pack, there appeared a small brown blur. The

Duke came past with ears laid back and teeth bared, afterburner blazing. Photo finish, the announcer said. There was a wait before the number went up. People were pounding me on the back. And it occurred to me that, for variety, and to spread our business around, we ought to run down to Nice for luncheon every week or so.

The fifth race was a long one, more than two and a half miles. Our choice was Lord of Lords. We were betting the owner, Pat O'Neill, and the trainer, whose name was Collet. The first time past he was out front by a length. But later, while the other horses were being unsaddled, Lord of Lords was still trying to find his way down the straightaway, wobbling so bad from side to side you'd have thought he'd stopped off at a wine tasting.

He wasn't why we left with two races left to run. Even Niarchos must lose a freighter from time to time. But it was cold and threatening rain. And with a horse race somewhere in the Paris area every day of the autumn season, getting rich isn't something you have to rush.

44

D ID YOU EVER set out deliberately to lose yourself in a forest? You simply choose an interesting direction and head that way until something—some stream or tangled thicket—deflects you. Or until some different and more inviting vista opens on another bearing.

One such aimless turn leads to the next. Your inner compass becomes useless. You lose any notion of your exact locus in the universe, and become just a creature afoot somewhere, your senses open, unencumbered by destination. It is an irresponsible feeling, and wonderfully free. All that is necessary is that you

125

have a fair idea of how to end the ramble when you want to; some confidence that you can, in fact, get out. Otherwise, adventure would soon give way to real alarm.

Seizing on the rarity of several consecutive sunny hours, that's how I lost myself in Paris one recent day. Even after several months, the city, with all its convoluted streets and improbable cornerings, still is a bit like a forest to me. The general arrangement of it I understand, and by taking my bearings on known landmarks I can stay oriented and keep the compass working. But between those landmarks, an uncharted wilderness lurks. So instead of being lost yet again accidentally, I decided to do it on purpose.

From the Place de l'Opéra, I struck first along the Boulevard des Capucines, then down the shop-crowded Rue Montmartre toward the Halles quarter and the soaring pile of stone, the Saint-Eustache Church, where I have read that Louis XIV took his first communion. All that was more or less familiar turf.

But then, turning through a twisting and narrow arcade, a covered passage, I was borne through and out into a quarter of entirely different character, along a teeming avenue to the Place de la Républic, where I'd been but once before. Then another way looked attractive, and I took that.

The sun went behind a cloud for a bit, so I hadn't the slightest idea which way I was headed. That new street led into a district that oddly combined peep shows and pornographic book stores with an array of splendid outdoor restaurants. The lunch hour came. The restaurant tables filled up with nice-looking folk who resolutely ignored the sex shops.

Surprisingly, then, the Halles and Saint-Eustache rose up in front again. Without knowing, I had traveled a wide circle. So I continued on past the Louvre and along the quay, crossing the Seine on the Pont Neuf and plunging into the maze of older, narrower *rues* and footways of the Latin Quarter. There is no use to bore you with the names of streets and alleys trod by someone who didn't know, or care, where he was going. Suffice that in six hours of walking you can cover a good deal of ground. But so rich is Paris, so varied a mix of distinct small neighborhoods, that not once in all that time did the scene grow repetitious.

On a corner somewhere a man asked street directions. He could not have found a less-qualified guide. He was Moroccan, a teacher of English literature from Casablanca, with only one day to spend here. For all his elegant mastery of French, he was as lost as I was.

He was looking for a store where he might buy presents for his wife and children, but we went to sit in a café instead. His place of birth, I discovered, was the exact scorched hamlet at the edge of the Sahara where once, more than 20 years ago, I was laid low by sickness. He quoted from Eugene O'Neill and Faulkner as if they were old friends. We exchanged addresses. His name was Abdellatif Fawzi. We invited one another to visit sometime in Casablanca and Kansas City—not likely to happen in either of our lives.

Then we finished our coffees and went separate ways back out into the maze.

On another street, a young woman of 17 or 18 years was speaking to passers-by, or trying to. Most just strode wordlessly on, as I meant to do. But I have daughters of nearly that age, so I stopped instead and asked if there was some problem. She was not French. She may have been from somewhere in the southern Mediterranean. Her face was a child's—but so beautiful it took the breath.

"I have no money," she said. "And I am not from here." She poured out some frightened tale about needing to meet her friend. If she only could manage to do that, the friend had a train ticket that would take her home. I didn't know if any of that was true. But I had 25 francs in my pocket, not quite three dollars in change, and gave her that.

She began suddenly to cry. I suppose her story was true, after all. I hurried away, embarrassed, and wished afterward that I'd had the sense to understand her plight more fully and perhaps steer her to better help. To wander the city aimlessly, lost by choice and able at any moment to find one's way, is one thing. But to be *really* lost in that forest, I thought, by bad luck or miscalculation, would be another.

So I turned and started back to where I thought I'd seen her. But I could not find the street.

45

E THNIC STEREOTYPES ARE usually unreliable and often cruelly unfair. But they persist nonetheless. They are one of the ways, however malicious or inexact, by which we try to catalogue in some understandable fashion the bewildering variety of human beings in the world.

Thus, Americans are held to be savagely materialistic, Germans warlike, Japanese inscrutable, Mexicans slothful, the English haughty, the Italians naughty and so forth. Hardly any national or racial group has escaped some such label. And while the stereotype may have some detectable root in history or observed behavior, usage transforms it into a tool of prejudice.

Frenchmen, according to this crude shorthand, are generally understood to be great lovers, their Latin natures aflame with ungovernable passion. As reputations go, that is not such a bad one to have. But like most of the others, it is greatly exaggerated. What Frenchmen are, as far as I can see, are irrepressible public *kissers*.

The vice is by no means epidemic even here. Some Frenchmen, obviously, have no wives, girlfriends or mistresses to kiss. There is a whole age group of older men, raised up on kissing hands, that got left behind—their puckers wasted—when hands went out in favor of more purposeful work. And of course there are a lot of others, under nine or 10, too young to have taken up the habit.

The practice of it seems to begin at about the time of the first facial eruptions and not to abate until well into the 20s, resuming then, briefly but with a vengeance, around that age—45 or so—when it becomes necessary to demonstrate before the world that one's powers are not declining.

There is nothing sly or secretive about it. You will be passing along a sidewalk in the full light of noon when, two or three steps ahead of you, some young couple will turn and cleave together with a bruising sound. And they will remain like that for minutes on end, either stock-still or trying to proceed in a clumsy, crablike way, while the flow of other pedestrians parts and passes on around, pulling shopping carts and carrying loaves of bread. Going for coffee the other afternoon, we let our attention wander for a moment and almost ran into such a pair, joined so solidly you'd have thought they'd gotten their braces caught. It happens without preamble or any warning. You just have to be alert for sidewalk kissers, as you are for the smaller obstacles left by people who walk their dogs.

The métro is another favored place—either in the cars themselves or, better, on the station platform at a busy hour, when a larger audience is assured. Last night I saw a truly spectacular performance, in which the principals were an oily-haired lad in a leather jacket and his anorexic-looking beloved wearing a knitted sweater and a look of bliss. Seizing her by the lapels of her sweater, he lifted the birdy creature straight off the ground and held her there, like a sack of laundry, their alimentary canals intricately joined.

It was late and the trains were running slowly. For most of a quarter-hour this show went on. I would like to say the star of it was blind with ardor and oblivious to all around him. But the truth is that, from time to time, he stole a look to be sure his feat of strength and imagination was receiving the attention it deserved. The several dozen of us on the platform looked at him and we looked at one another. And it was only by a miracle of restraint that we did not break into a round of outright applause.

My suspicion, despite all these virile displays, is that the reputation of Frenchmen as insatiable romantics and gifted seducers is overdrawn, as most stereotypes are, and that they probably do about the same amount of kissing as people anywhere. The difference is that they prefer to have people watching. It seems to take an audience to inflame them. And that, to my lights, is not romance. That is strange, strange, strange.

46

EVERY DAY IT RAINS, and these are not the refreshing showers of a gentler season, or even the transient squalls of only a month ago. They are continuous and vertical and cold.

Smoke seen curling from the chimneys of other blocks of flats suggests that, in those buildings, someone has fired the boilers up. But not in ours. Searching the apartment, we have found two grates high up against the ceiling—two three-by-six-inch grates, for five rooms and a hall—from which heat may eventually come. But nothing issues from them yet. Rain hammers at the window glass. The chill seeps through the walls and under the cracks of the sills.

Yesterday I went early to the Rue Monge on the Left Bank to drink a coffee with my friend, Soyam, after his duty ended at the Hôtel de France. He did us an astonishing kindness our first

Soyam

night in Paris—gave his own small apartment to use when there was not a hotel room to be had anywhere in the city. Now I like seeing him from time to time. His goodness is inspiring.

Soyam is the night clerk, and is supposed to be free at 9 o'clock in the morning. But the kitchen maid had not appeared for work, so besides managing the desk he had to carry breakfasts to the rooms. Lodgers came to give their keys or pay their accounts, then went out with umbrellas drawn low over their heads. The telephone switchboard buzzed as others woke and demanded their trays. All the competing duties this small brown man performed in his deft and soft-mannered way. And at 10 o'clock, an hour after his time, he was able at last to leave.

We walked up the Rue Monge in the rain and took a table inside a café. The coffees and croissants were set before us, and as we talked it was soon plain, though he tried to pretend cheerfulness, that his spirit was low.

Soyam is from the small island of Mauritius in the sunny Indian Ocean. The unending cold rain, he admitted, had oppressed him. But there was something else and worse—a "great problem," as he described it. In brief outline, it was this. A young Mauritian woman, a girl of hardly more than 20 years, whose family was known to Soyam's, had come as an *au pair* to a Paris couple, to do work in the household and look after the two children. It is the way many girls from North Africa, the Indies and elsewhere manage to make their way to France, and the opportunities they imagine here.

The woman of this couple was a journalist, and her work took her often out of the city for days at a time. In the small hour of a night during one such absence, the man, who was 45 years old, knocked at the door of the *au pair*. Frightened, alone in this vast foreign place, she yielded to him. Other nights there were more knocks. The fear receded. And soon, I gathered from Soyam's telling of it, she yielded with some enthusiasm. But not, evidently, without guilt. For somehow she found my friend, her countryman, and told him of the situation. And because of the acquaintance of their families, he felt in some way responsible.

"I told her she must leave," he said. "Go away from there. I told her to consider her future. With such a man, married, with 45 years, there is no future."

The girl did leave that household. And Soyam arranged for her to stay with his friend, another young Mauritian woman. But the man obtained her address and telephone—in all likelihood she gave them to him. So the liaisons continued in the friend's room, when the friend was away at work.

"For more than a month, now—" Soyam said, staring at his undrunk coffee, "—for nearly two months, I am very uneasy in my heart. I take pills to sleep. I have no appetite for food. My weight becomes less."

"I'm sorry," I said.

"I think of my sisters in Mauritius. They are very straight and correct. I know this because they are almost like my daughters. I have raised them. And this girl was like that. But what must I do? If I beat her, it may do no good. Sometimes I think that I will telephone to that man's house and speak to his wife, but maybe she would not believe me. Or he might kill me then. It is possible. So you see it is a very great problem. And I cannot sleep, wondering what I must do."

"I don't know," I said to him, because I really didn't. "But in the street there—" We looked out at the cobbles, shiny in the rain. "In the street there must be a thousand problems. And in the city, like any big city, there must be a million of them."

Just then, as if to confirm the truth of it, a sad transvestite went past on the sidewalk outside the café window—a drenched figure in a bronze evening gown, hair done up in a bun behind, with a two-day stubble of black beard. In a cold rain, Bohemian Paris can be less amusing.

"You can't solve all the problems," I told him. "You're not big enough."

The apparition turned onto the Rue Mirbel and disappeared around a building corner. Soyam looked at the rain running in cold streams down the window.

"Yes," he said. "I will try to remember that." But, good as he is, I suppose that he will not.

47

AMERICANS DO NOT LIVE with quite the same appreciation Europeans have of how fragile is the tissue that passes for civility among nations, or of how suddenly, how ruinously, it can be torn. War, though we are no strangers to it, has a different meaning for us.

It is an event that happens in some other place, and that young men go away to, for reasons that are politically explainable or not. And afterward come home from—or not. The lucky ones are greeted by no scene of general devastation. They walk the same streets and pass the same houses as before. The unlucky, even if the cause they died for was misguided or unpopular, eventually are memorialized. And, except for those who mourn them, life will not have been much changed by any of this. The nation turns matter-of-factly to other business. The war passes finally into that realm of enormities—presidential assassinations, earthquakes in Turkey, famine in Africa—made bearable by the sterility of remembered headlines.

In this century, at least, that's how wars have been for us. But not for Europeans. Not for the French.

Go northwest three hours by car from Paris in a warmer season, for pleasure at the seaside, and the beaches you come to will be ones where, in the memory of people not yet old, tens of thousands died. The ground still is cratered, the cement gun emplacements still there, empty but otherwise unaffected by the elapse of so few years. Six hours by express train in the other direction will bring a Frenchman to the river across which, twice in one lifetime, his country's destroyers came. The people on that river's far bank are friends now. The French say it with an earnestness they want believed.

The trouble is that Europe's memories are neither distant nor abstract. In a métro station here, covering a wall, you find inscribed the names of employees of the transport service of that district—hundreds of them—who perished not for some far-off principle but for the very survival of France. The same in post offices and railway stations.

Affixed to the buildings along public streets are little plaques, sometimes with vases for flowers beside or below, telling by name who lost his or her life there—in that exact place—and on what day, and sometimes as a result of what specific act of patriotism or valor. Pass beside farm fields in open country, or through the squares of backwater farming villages, and you come upon more of the endless monuments, their messages all very much the same: *To our heroes, dead for France.* Followed by yet another list of names. And though the lives to which those names attached are perfectly unknown to you, just the numbers are affecting.

That has been the meaning of war to a Frenchman, to any European. It is not something you have to go away to—not very far, at any rate. War comes to you. Villages, whole cities, disappear in cataclysmic bombardment. Families are extinguished, the young and the old impartially. And when the sound of the cannons has subsided, suffering of a different and longer kind begins. And more often than not, the map of the continent has changed.

Washington may be the capital of the West, at least of western power, as Moscow and Bejing are the capitals of the East. But to live here, at an ocean's remove, is to better

135

understand why it is that the Europeans, and the French in particular, can sometimes be such nettlesome allies.

Their whole history tells them how often the tissue of peace has torn, and how easily it could again. The war we replay in our nightmares—the one that will leave neither memories nor any rememberers—does not preoccupy them as intimately as the lesser one that could be fought across this same scarred piece of earth. They have buried whole generations of their young. We have not. They have heard the pounding of alien armies through their streets. We have not. Now they are invited to risk the future on the will and the judgments of other men whose experience, whose perspective, is different from their own. As again, by the luck of our history, we have not had to do.

In the politics of war or survival, it is only our innocence they mistrust.

48

HUNTING WAS THE noble sport, conducted over vast domains from which the woodcutters were kept at bay. So the French have royalty to thank for their prosperity of surviving forests, which in this season are wonderfully deep and mysterious and alive.

The wild boar and the stag still harbor there, along with hares and ermines and partridges and lesser creatures. And the French in the dark of autumn still go to the woods for the hunt, but for a prize of another sort. For it is there, in the undisturbed humus of the leaf-fall of slow centuries, that one finds a delicacy so enchanting to the national palate, its lure if anything enhanced by a faint peril of mortality. The quarry is the *champignon sauvage,* the wild mushroom.

In Changing Light

So fecund is the moist floor of the autumn forest, canopied by ancient oaks and chestnuts and pines, that fungi thrive in a profusion rarely to be seen. Hardly a step can be taken without treading on one or several. And their variety seems endless. There are orange and yellow ones with caps turned up at the edges, making bowls to hold the perpetual drip of the rain. There are nut-brown ones, small-capped and symmetrical, occurring in fairy rings. There are gray ones, and some nearly black. And still others so white that, seen in the half-light of the woods, they seem almost to be encompassed by a halo.

Until you have seen it, you hardly can imagine such an uncontainable vigor of things erupting in the gloom and decay. They burst up through the leaves—you almost imagine that you can hear them coming, shouldering the mulch of ages aside. They have their moment of flowering and, in another day, are themselves covered over by the white fur of humbler fungi, and go back to the soil again.

How I wish I could spend a day in those woods with my friend, Ansel Stubbs, and by this I tell him so. His company would be fine on many counts: the good conversation, his counsel in wines, the stories he would share. Live 100 years, as he has, and you know a lot of things worth telling. But what I would most value in the woods would be his advice on mushrooms, about which he is a published authority.

Some of the ones to be gathered there are much prized by cooks and cost as much as 170 francs a kilo, more than eight dollars a pound, if you can find them in a town market. And though I have not tried them, they are said to send the eater into transports of delight. The problem is that other varieties, very similar to the untrained eye, provide transport of a different and more final kind. Unless you know absolutely which one is which, it is better not to trifle with the *champignon sauvage* and to settle, instead, for the blander supermarket kind.

But in the matter of mushrooms, the French are a nation of

risk-takers. So that on any outing into the countryside this time of year, you find their cars parked along the road shoulder at the woods' edge—lines of cars, in the favored places. And presently you will see whole families emerge from the groves and thickets, plastic shopping bags fat with their harvest, all smiling and laughing as if it never crossed their minds that the next meal might send them promptly off to the great auberge in the sky.

Every season, as you might expect, there are mistakes made, some of them with tragic result. The hazard is common enough that, in mushroom time, the pharmacies display in their windows poster-sized identification charts. And they also keep on duty—are required by law to do it, I've been told—someone qualified to say what's edible and what is not. If you come there and empty the contents of your collecting sack on the counter, the druggist will, as a service, cull out the deadly from the delicious.

I took a ramble in one of those forests the other day. There were mushrooms everywhere and, for just a moment, I was tempted. But then I decided my affairs were not sufficiently in order, my appetite not quite that great.

The druggist on the circle of our street I gladly depend on for various ointments and antacids. I do not for a moment impugn his ability or training. But as a matter of strict personal policy, no mushrooms pass my lips that have not first been classified and approved by my adviser on edible fungi. And since Ansel Stubbs is an ocean and half a continent away, I will never know what rapture I may have missed.

49

THE FEAR OF BURGLARY, and not only in our building, is frankly obsessive. Many insurance companies, we are told, will not honor their policies unless the place broken into can be shown to have been protected by a specified number of locks, usually three to every door.

The locks are elaborate, each fitted with a different key. As the various keys are turned, tumblers fall, pistons slide, dead bolts retract from their steel sockets and, in due time, entry is gained. The sound of someone admitting himself to his own apartment is like visitors' day at a maximum-security prison. Our door has but two locks—one small and one large, the large one operated by what looks like a key to the castle keep. So by local standards we are pitifully undersecured, practically inviting pillage. Based on our experience of last night, however, one lock is entirely sufficient.

We were going to dinner with friends. Our daughters had made plans to see a movie with their schoolmates. We all struck off on our separate ways just as families do anywhere—breathlessly, already late for our engagements, with hardly time for a civil word between us. Our friends were waiting at their hotel. And as they and we set out for the restaurant, I felt in my pocket for a métro ticket.

"You have your key, haven't you?" I asked my wife.

"No," she said. "Don't you have yours?"

One of the girls must have taken a key, we decided. Anyway, it was just the key to the small lock we needed. The heavy lock we throw only for longer absences. Dinner passed merrily. It got to be half past 10 o'clock. Our family reassembled at the apartment—on the landing outside the door. The girls did *not* have keys.

"Madame Freguin will have one," I said. The concierge of

the building customarily keeps a spare, in case of emergency. Then we remembered that we had already gotten the extra key from her a couple of weeks before, and had forgotten to return it. It was locked inside with the other three. Luckily, the Freguins had not yet retired. So I rang their first-floor bell and explained the problem. Madame Freguin's husband, Jean-Pierre, knew the procedure exactly. First he called the police, to report that my door would have to be opened by extraordinary means. Then he telephoned a locksmith.

"It's just the small lock," I said. "Probably he can open it with some kind of passkey."

"Perhaps," Jean-Pierre said, but without much enthusiasm. He knows something about French door locks.

It had gotten on toward midnight, so I waited outside the front door of the building to admit the locksmith. The traffic on the street thinned. The grill at the métro entrance closed. The last bus went by. The locksmith came at 1 o'clock, and said his car had given him a problem on the way. He got out a promising looking box—big enough to contain a thousand skeleton keys—and we went up on the elevator to the dark landing, where my family was sleeping against a wall. The locksmith opened his box and got out a heavy-duty power drill and an arsenal of metal bits.

"But you can see," I said, "it's just a little lock."

He located an electrical outlet, plugged in his cord, aimed the drill bit at the center of the lock and leaned into his work. Metal screamed against metal. The wall of our apartment, and of the other apartments on the landing, began to resonate sonorously. I could imagine, though I couldn't see, our neighbors springing startled from their beds and the lights going on in their rooms. I could feel myself riveted by the eyes through the peepholes of their doors.

Between his drillings, the locksmith whistled gaily—a happy craftsman—and discoursed loudly on the excellence of the lock.

"Five pistons," he cried admiringly. *"Five!* You see? It will not yield."

It did yield, of course. Even mountains crumble in time. Sweating from his exertions, he finally used a hammer to drive a screwdriver into the opening he had cut, then used a wrench to turn the screwdriver. And a few minutes after 2 o'clock in the morning, our door swung open. He would have to return sometime today to install a replacement lock, he explained, since he'd brought no other with him. But we still had one lock remaining on the door—the big one that turns with the castle key.

"Perhaps that will be enough," he said. "For one night."

"Probably so," I agreed, having already struck any risk of burglary from my list of future concerns.

50

ONE IS ASSAILED, periodically, by what may best be described as *linguistic fatigue.* The effort of reproducing the sounds and constructions of the alien tongue grows insupportable. Concentration falters. You seem to have forgotten what little you knew. There is a sudden, lonely sense of being submerged in a meaningless babble which it was preposterous to have imagined you ever would understand.

Fortunately, these episodes are brief. But they are demoralizing—all the more if words happen to be the music of your life.

Not long ago, for example, I had to write a check to a tradesman for some small repair here at the apartment. Two mornings later he appeared again at the door, saying there was a problem about the check. I first understood him to mean the bank had refused to honor it. When, in fact, what he was trying to explain was that he had lost the check and wanted me to write him another.

A quarter-hour it took to clarify that. Then the bank had to be called. The check, it turned out, had been found by someone in the street and was being returned by mail. Payment would be stopped on it, in order that I might issue a duplicate to the workman, who stood at my elbow during this labored conversation, probably wishing by then he'd just written off the loss and gotten on with his life. The bank required that the whole affair be recapitulated in a letter confirming the stop-payment order. So after the tradesman left, that meant most of another hour with grammar texts, dictionary and a verb wheel. Half a day had been lost, and I was left feeling stupid and exhausted.

The only remedy in such times is to speak one's own language for a while. What's talked about is unimportant. It is enough just to be reassured that you have not lost, for good, the capacity to make your thoughts understood, your needs known.

Le Clap's Bar, in the next block of the street, is a dive of little distinction. It's a haunt, especially in the evening, of serious drinkers. From time to time, one of Le Clap's clients can be seen to emerge, position himself with a hand against a parked car for support, and, with the solemnity of someone performing a sacrament, void his stomach at the curb. But in times of moral crisis, like after the business of the wayward check, I sometimes stop in there for a coffee because the bartender speaks English. He learned it during seven years as a croupier in a London casino, and is happy for the chance to practice.

He sets my coffee before me and, because the daytime trade is light, usually draws one for himself. Our conversations are about nothing profound, but they are intensely satisfying.

The job at the casino was a good one, he said the other day. He wishes sometimes he had not left it to come home to Paris. There must have been great responsibility handling all that money, I observed. "You had to be careful," he said. "Always careful. But there was not so much pressure as this."

I looked around the place. There were only two customers besides myself—a man standing at the far end of the bar, reading the horse-racing paper, and a young woman alone at a table, looking into her glass of red wine. The pressure did not seem to me unbearable.

"Yes, in the day it is all right," he said. "People come in to take their coffee and a croissant. Or to have a glass of something. Two glasses, maybe. But at night—" He shook his head. "You hear all their stories. The same ones every time, and sometimes more than once in a night. It is noisy. My head hurts. I have been here from half past six in the morning, and it is now 11 o'clock at night. I want to go home. And they say, 'Pour my glass. Let me tell you again about my life.' Now *that* is pressure."

So too much talk—even in one's own language—can be as punishing as too little.

He spoke about the cost of cars, and of insurance for them. And about a headline in my paper, folded on the bar, telling of another fall in the price of oil, of which he approved. And of a woman he knows who lives on a barge, moored at the bank of the Seine nearby, with central heating and a dozen cats. Glad as he is to use his English, the effort tires him after while. The woman with the barge and cats he told about in French. And I found, to my surprise, that I could understand him—could even make reasonable reply.

"Do you want another coffee?" he asked.

"No, but I'll come back again."

"Always in the daytime," he said. "Daytime is best."

Outside, on the street, the babble had resolved itself into sensible discourse again.

·

51

LOSE YOUR DAUGHTER of tender age in a foreign city of nearly 8 million souls and, I promise you, your definition of terror will have to be revised.

My wife was abroad on an errand. The girls had stayed for some activity at their school, 10 minutes away by bus. And I, groggy from lunch and from having written late the night before, was napping on the couch until friends arrived to go for an afternoon walk and then to supper at a restaurant nearby. When I woke, my wife was home. And soon after that the older daughter appeared. Her sister was not with her.

"That's queer," the older one said, "because she left on the bus before I did." A small mystery, but not alarming. Probably she had stopped off to visit with a friend, or to look in shop windows. They have reached that age where things seen behind the glass in clothing stores hold lethal and expensive fascination.

Our friends came, then, and we set off on our excursion through a park. We would look in again before going to the restaurant, to put our minds at rest. No doubt we would find her bent over her homework, with some logical excuse for tardiness. "She's spirited," I said as we walked. "But she's quite responsible, in her way."

The light failed. We came back along the street in darkness, and turned the key in the door, knowing she would have some reasonable story to tell.

"She still isn't here," her sister said. It was 7 o'clock—long past the hour for innocent loitering. A shudder passed through us all. Suddenly this city, in which we've come to feel at home and most times perfectly at ease, seemed as immense and labyrinthine as some mapless jungle in which unnamed hazards lurked.

"How was it, living a while in Paris?" I could imagine people

144

asking. And us saying, "Oh, very nice, very interesting. Yes, I'd have to say that, on the whole, we liked Paris very much. Except, of course, as you may have heard, we lost one of the children there."

We found the telephone number of her friend, a girl in the class, written on a paper in her room. The mother answered, a gentle and caring woman with whom we had spoken before, and we explained the problem. Then the friend got on the phone, but could shed no light on the matter. When she'd gotten off the bus, only our daughter and two or three others still were aboard, one of them a boy named Nelson.

The friend's mother was by now weeping with alarm. "It's such a *big* city," she was saying. That had occurred to us.

We telephoned this Nelson individual, and again got the mother. Nelson wasn't there. He'd come home hours ago, alone. And had gone off to the Paris auto show with a couple of his friends from the neighborhood to look at cars. Was it possible our daughter could be with them? She was quite certain not. It was plain from her tone of voice that she did not think of her Nelson, at age 15 or so, as a rake and despoiler.

Maybe we would just go there and have a look, we suggested.

"It's up to you," she said. "But it's a big exposition. There must be 20,000 people there."

Never mind dinner, our friends said considerately. How could they help? Should we involve the police at this point? Or should we set out first to comb the city? If you have ever been in Paris, or even looked at a map of it, you know how many small and crooked streets there are, what warrens of ancient and leaning buildings, how many lightless doorways into which an innocent might be drawn.

My wife went into the girls' room to hear from our surviving daughter one more time the story of the bus, on the chance there might be in that some clue we'd overlooked. In a minute she was back.

145

"She's found," my wife said. We sprang collectively to our feet. "She's in her bed." The beds are bunk beds, and hers is the upper one—with a high wooden rail around it. She'd been lying very flat there, under a puffy comforter. "I saw the corner of the comforter move," my wife said. "And I thought it was a cat. Then I remembered we don't have any cats here."

The object of all this concern appeared then, eyes full of sleep, amazed and a bit pleased at her sudden notoriety.

"What time is it?" she asked.

Half past seven, we told her.

"I've been asleep four hours."

Who'd let her in the apartment, I demanded to know.

"You did. I had to ring the bell three times."

Vaguely, then, I did remember being disturbed once from my rest on the couch—but not for what, or by whom.

"Well, we were lucky," I said. *"This time."* If you are a parent, you know how quickly relief translates to anger.

"What do you mean, *lucky?* I was asleep in my bed."

"I don't care," I snapped. "It's a big city, Paris. Eight million people. It's a jungle out there. We're going to have to take a whole new look at the rules around this house. We can't go through this again."

"I was in my bed," she said once more, as if that were any excuse.

"We'll talk about it tomorrow," I told her.

We went out then with our friends to the restaurant and had a simple meal for whose excellence I cannot account, unless it was the lively talk and a tasty bottle of wine.

52

IT WAS THE EVENING rush hour, with a cold rain pelting. We had gone out under our umbrella on an errand to the store. And as we crossed with the pedestrian light at our corner—the same corner where we have previously seen bicycles and motorcycles hit—a car made a U-turn in the intersection and ran down a woman in the street.

It happened only steps from us, and in terrible slow-motion, as accidents do. The car wheeled suddenly around, too near the crosswalk. The woman saw it coming, but not in time. She dropped her umbrella and shopping sack. Then the car struck her, bore her several feet and flung her down. Hearing the impact, the driver stopped. The woman, her leg bloodied, sprawled in a muddy puddle, making a high, moaning cry of desolation. The driver, a young man, sprang out of his machine, grasped her under the arm of her raincoat and was trying to pull her to her feet. But the injured leg gave way and she fell back into the wetness. The young man began to gesture and berate her, not in meanness but in panic.

The French do not make much fuss about accidents, perhaps because they happen so often. In the two others we have observed, standard procedure seemed to be simply to pick up the fallen and, if they and their machines still were reasonably mobile, to brush them off and send them on their way, never minding the question of fault.

But this woman was plainly hurt. One man showed momentary interest. Then all the rest of the rush-hour pedestrians went marching on about their errands. It seemed an unfair contest, somehow—the woman bleeding, wide-eyed with fright and despair, being shouted at by the equally-frightened driver. So while my wife went inside to ask a shopkeeper to telephone for ambulance and police, I gathered up her few scattered things and assisted her to the safety of the curb.

The car belonged to an auto rental agency just down the street, where the young driver was employed. Another man from there soon arrived and together, balancing the rule of never moving a victim against the nature of her hurt and the inclemency of the night, we helped her to a chair inside the agency's office.

The manager of the agency suggested she might just prefer to be driven directly home.

"No," she said sensibly. "I will wait for the police."

In 25 minutes an ambulance appeared, and the medics went considerately, capably, about determining the extent of her injury. Five minutes after the ambulance, the lawyer for the rental company arrived. And five minutes behind the lawyer came the police, who seemed to have gotten lost.

Meantime, the young man who was driving the car had refined his account. Instead of crossing with the pedestrian signal, the woman had been wandering aimlessly out in traffic. Instead of his hitting her, she had slipped and fallen in front of his car. He was not lying in a deliberate way. His memory was simply reconstructing the event as he wished it had happened. Probably he even believed this less-damning version himself.

I wrote out our address and phone number and gave it to the woman before she was loaded onto a stretcher in the ambulance. "In case it is needed," I told her.

The lawyer was trying to joke with the police about the triviality of the event, while the young man was drawing out his version of it on a piece of paper. By now, in the drawing, the woman was almost directly in the center of the street.

"You saw it?" the shorter of the two policemen asked me. I replied that I had. We went out under my umbrella to the intersection, where I showed him how it had happened. Then we went back to the shelter of the office. He made note of the information from our passports, and also our address and telephone number.

The taller policeman had taken off his hat, seated himself at the office desk and opened a pad of forms for his report.

"Surely you're not going to make a paper on this poor *garçon*"—this unfortunate boy—"for so small a thing," the lawyer said. He was a big man in a gray suit and necktie.

The policeman leaned around him to point at me. "But that man saw it." The lawyer did not bother turning to look. He was persistent, but jocular, as if it were something about which sensible minds could easily come to an understanding.

"This *garçon* has a family. He has a wife and children. For so small a thing, surely —"

The policeman gestured in my direction again.

"That man saw it," he repeated tiredly, and continued to write on his form.

I would not presume that the relationship between French barristers and the police is as it is in some other Latin countries. Nor do I bear any ill will toward the driver, who was only behaving as frightened young men do. But victims also need representation. And so, in some abstract way, does truth. And I was struck suddenly by the unworthy suspicion that, except for our having witnessed it, the accident might not have occurred at all.

"We have your telephone number," the small policeman said. "So that is all. We can call you any time."

"Any time," I said. It will be interesting to see if they do.

53

Many things work here, and a few of them work very well. Public transit, for one, works wonderfully. Trains shuttle millions of riders through the tunnels. Buses ply the traffic-clotted streets and somehow arrive, on the far side of the city, within a minute or two of the posted time. Recently, in some dispute over cost-of-living increases, transit employees staged a one-day slowdown. Parisians were warned to brace for terrible inconvenience, perhaps even municipal paralysis. But there was no hardship. Even at half-speed, the Paris transit system is so far superior to most American ones at their best that the slowdown was scarcely noticed.

Escalators work—a good one-half to two-thirds of the time. So do the banks, though with maddening deliberation. The telephone usually works, provided the call you are wanting to make is not urgent. Or provided you can find one on the street from which the dial mechanism has not been ripped out or the cord of the earpiece amputated.

Even the French postal service works in its own mysterious way. Stand in the line at the post office to buy stamps or dispatch a package and you would swear that the people behind the desks and counters are dead or drugged. You have seen more life than that in a wax museum. Yet the service *must* work. For once you have managed to get letters posted, they do seem to find their way abroad. And most mornings Madame Freguin slips an envelope or two under the apartment door.

Coin-operated photo machines, on the other hand, *never* work. You might not regard it as critical. But in a society whose bureaucratic wheels are oiled by passport-sized photographs, this breakdown in the mechanical order is of no small consequence.

The French have a passion for documentation. In order to

obtain identity papers, a monthly métro pass, work permit, railroad discount card or any number of other certifications of entitlement, it is necessary to produce photographs of oneself ranging in quantity from one to eight. Automated booths to provide these pictures are positioned ubiquitously in métro and train stations and major stores around the city. Theoretically, you enter the booth, crank the seat to the desired height, put seven francs in the slot, wait for the strobe to flash. And four minutes later you will be presented a set of likenesses, gummy to the touch, showing a protohominid with purple flesh tones and a two-inch forehead.

But that is only theory. Of the several hundred such machines in Paris, on a given day not more than one or two of them will be found in working order. The others will have been tinkered with, jammed, abused or otherwise put out of commission. Sometimes they just swallow your coins without comment or performance. More often there is a sign warning of their unwillingness to *marche*—that is, to operate. All these idle machines must generate very little revenue for the concessionaire. But there is a fortune to be made in printing the signs that say they are broken.

Rumors circulate quickly in a city of this size. Someone will mention hearing of a photomat in operation at the Pont de Sevres métro station. There will be a sudden detectable population drift toward that quarter of town. Arriving, you will find an impatient line at the booth. At the front of the line will be a man without any photos, beating on the coin return, trying to get his seven francs back. Then someone will flash a promising bulletin about the booth at the Franklin Delano Roosevelt station. And everyone will rush off to there, only to find the apparatus disemboweled by a technician who says he doesn't know *when* it might be back in service or if, indeed, it can ever be caused to work again.

Luckily, our passports are valid and our visas are in order.

151

However there is a further official document we have been advised to obtain, without which we are apt to be regarded as wetbacks who floated up the Seine on inner tubes. I have forgotten what month it was that we first set out to try to qualify for that paper. Anyway, it was weeks and weeks ago.

Eight pictures of each adult family member are demanded with the application. One bureau directed us to another office, which directed us to a man who offered to make the photos for a price *five times* what they would cost from a machine. We thanked him, and stumbled back out to follow the crowds to yet another métro station. Now we have substantially given up on the paper in question.

This city must be full of undocumented folks, their strength sapped and their will broken by failed attempts to have their pictures taken. When the time finally comes that the authorities knock on our door, maybe they will believe our story and maybe they will not. But if photos are required for our deportation, it will be their problem, not ours.

54

COMING UP THE STAIR from a pedestrian underpass one recent morning, I met a man in a flowered gown who was handing out cards to anyone who would take them. And since I never turn down something offered free, even if it is only a slip of paper, I stuck it in my pocket. Coming across it later, I found that it was the business card of one Monsieur Diaby Sekou, whose services it spelled out in detail.

Monsieur Sekou, it seems, is a member of the Order of African Marabouts—a certified authority of 15 years experience in all matters psychological, telepathic and clairvoyant, an expert in the use of mysterious plants well known in the Great Sacred Forest and a specialist in dealing with desperate concerns that may appear otherwise unsolvable. The answers to any questions I might have about the past, present or future—whether concerning work, health or love—Monsieur Sekou would reveal to my stupefaction (that was his word for it, my *stupefaction*) if only I would come to see him between the hours of 8 A.M. and 9 P.M. at his apartment on the far side of the city.

Having questions in some of those areas, as most of us do, but not all that eager to be stupefied, I laid the slip of paper aside. But I have since learned that the profession of marabout is a crowded one. Because on subsequent days, on different corners, I have been handed the cards of Monsieur Sekou's competitors.

The fellows giving these out are not, I believe, the sorcerers themselves, who most likely are back in the clutter of their *ateliers,* surrounded by herbs and spiders and pickled snakes and other equipage brought from the Sacred Forest, waiting to stupefy. These are only their attendants and apprentices and shills, out drumming up business on the street.

One of the other cards was from Monsieur Dramé, researcher into matters of romance, business, family problems, sport, school examinations and luck. Monsieur Dramé's services include "the inspiration of remarkable sexual desire" and also protection against all sorts of bad influences—the latter being essential, I should think, if Monsieur Dramé were successful on the first count.

His results, according to the card, are miraculous. How "miraculous" stacks up against "stupefying" I can't say. For the convenience of his clients, he will undertake to solve problems by mail. Correspondence is invited from anywhere in the world. All that is necessary is to send your name, photograph, birth date, the nature of your request and a stamped envelope, and Monsieur Dramé will get right to work on it. I see certain dangers in that. Suppose Monsieur Dramé keeps a messy office.

Suppose, say, that he got a letter from a gentleman with scant libido in Toledo mixed up with a letter from a matron in Toronto, seeking advice about her investments in porcelain. A couple of months later—for reasons her family or the police would be at a loss to explain—she would leap up and go bellowing along the boulevard in a rage of ungovernable lust.

The third card was from Monsieur Dansoko Abdoulaye, knowledgeable in the magic both of Africa and the West, reader of Tarots, performer of divinations, dispeller of charms and curses. His card is the least inviting, printed on flimsy paper with one telephone number marked out and another penciled in. It is lean on specific information, and offers no promise of results, either miraculous or stupefying. It does mention, vaguely and rather ominously it seems to me, his occasional resort to something called the Ritual of the Seven Candles. I wouldn't go near Monsieur Abdoulaye on a bet.

Why all these invitations have been handed me in the space of a few days I can't explain. Maybe it was just chance. Or maybe, as the season closes down, people tend to dwell more on their troubles and, consequently, the business of marabouts and *voyants* picks up. Anyhow, I have put their cards away for safe keeping in a compartment of the desk. I do not have any immediate, large problems needing attention. If one happens to come up, I am assured that, though far from home, I will not be without spiritual advice.

One question occurs, though. There's a horse race some-where every day in Paris this time of year. Why, if Messrs. Sekou, Dramé and Abdoulaye can see the future as clearly as they claim, are they sitting home with their herbs and pickled snakes? Why don't I ever see them at the track?

55

THE EMBASSY OF INDIA is set among handsome townhouses on a short, quiet street that dead-ends beside a park, the Jardin du Ranelagh, in the fashionable 16th arrondissement. And it was there, at 7 o'clock of a perfect autumn morning, that word of the assassination in New Delhi was received.

On the stage of world politics there had been two "iron ladies," both of them targets of hatred by minorities under their rule. A little more than a fortnight before, one of them, Margaret Thatcher, the British prime minister, had narrowly escaped death in the bombing of her Brighton hotel by Irish Republican Army terrorists.

Indira Gandhi, premier of India, was less lucky. Twenty days before her 67th birthday, 18 years after first taking leadership of her troubled and barely-governable country, she had been murdered at close quarters by two members of her personal bodyguard—members also of the rebellious Sikh community. Few other details were immediately known.

The wet Paris autumn had given way to a spell of golden days. After hearing the first radio bulletin, I went to the embassy to see what more might be learned. The way there led through the park, aflame with color, and through an iron gate at the end of the Rue Alfred Dehodencq.

Three Indian men, officials of the embassy, were standing together on the sidewalk in front of the building. Their manner was confused and still a bit disbelieving.

"Evidently it is true," one of them said. "But we have no more information." Black limousines of the diplomatic corps had just begun to arrive, unloading on the drive, then turning to wait at the end of the short street.

Who was expected to succeed her as leader of the country? Would it be her remaining son, Rajiv Gandhi?

"We know nothing," one of the officials said. "The party must consult. Parliament must act. We only listen to the radio, as you do. It is impossible to make any statement so soon."

Several uniformed French police arrived then to take up station along the street, but so unobtrusively that people coming out of the townhouses and joggers panting through the crisp morning did not notice. The news seemed still generally unknown.

(The first newspaper headlines of the tragedy would not be on the streets until afternoon. Then, in a café, a man would snatch the paper from my hand and cry out, in dismay, "Gandhi! Is it so?" He was Pakistani, he said. "But when there is change in India, we fear the future.")

The Indian community in Paris, unlike London's, is fairly small—several hundred at most. Yet through the late morning and on into afternoon, singly and in solemn groups, small dark-skinned, dark-suited men could be seen crossing the park and turning through the gate into the Rue Dehodencq. Leaves were spinning down in a yellow rain. Children were kicking soccer balls across the grass, and people had spread blankets to take the gift of the brilliant autumn day. In a corner of the park a little circus had raised its single tent, and lions were slumbering in cages turned to the sun.

After coming back through the gate from their visits to the embassy, the Indian men seemed in no hurry to leave. Hands clasped behind their backs, heads inclined in quiet conversation, they walked in twos and threes in the dappled sunlight, or sat together on benches. The setting was wonderfully serene, but their thoughts, one could be sure, were far away from here—in a part of the world where civility is fragile, where one death can soon mean thousands more.

A call to the French foreign ministry later in the day confirmed it. Across India, already, the violence had begun.

56

THERE REALLY ARE only two wisdoms to be gotten by entering through the narrow iron gate at No. 1 Place Denfert-Rochereau and descending the spiral stairway of chiseled stone. Both wisdoms are profoundly reassuring. The first is that the river of life has run very long and very strong. The second is that, after one has swum one's own short moment in it, the current can be trusted to bear safely, surely on. Until now, at any rate, it always has.

For at the bottom of that winding stair, along the galleries of ancient quarries from which were cut the stones to build the early city, are stored the bones of some 6 million Parisians of all the ages. The Municipal Ossuary, the place is antiseptically called. And it supplies the answer to that macabre question that has gnawed at many a childish imagination: *What happens when all the cemeteries fill up?*

Occupy a city long enough and that happens. It happened in Paris for a fact. After 1,000 years of burials in the cemetery of the Innocents, the strata of layered dead had risen eight feet above the surrounding grade. It is said that there were "accidents" in the certain cellars of the adjoining neighborhood—the nature of those best not too much dwelt on. The living begged the authorities for protection from the dead. In the 60 years it took the bureaucracy to act, another whole generation had made its contribution to the problem. But finally, during 15 months in 1786 and 1787, the Innocents was emptied—the bones, it is recorded, being transported to the quarries in carts at dusk, followed by chanting priests. From then through 1814, more cemeteries were abolished and their lands reclaimed.

For the last 110 years the Municipal Ossuary, or *les catacombes,* as the place is commonly called, has been open to the public. And even in this city of endless wonders, it remains a durable attraction. You might suppose that an excursion down into those subterranean halls would be, if not exactly horrifying, at least a trifle melancholy. But that's not so. Death, in the singular, has a power to startle and sadden. It seems an unnatural and lonely affair. But death in such numbers, happening over centuries and by infirmities and violences long forgotten, is different. One feels a witness to a most logical and natural process. And the reflections it evokes are of a longer and less personal kind—rather like the wistfulness one feels upon looking at the stalks and dried seed pods of an autumn-blasted summer garden.

Moreover, the laborers charged with carrying out the relocation of two centuries ago were not without some artistry and humor. The larger bones—femurs and fibulas and such—are racked up neatly between the stone pillars that support the quarry roof. Skulls provide the accent pieces, in decorative lines and borders or sometimes arranged to form some figure such as a cross.

And, again, I have to say that it is neither chilling nor repellent. In that place, mortality seems just another fact, neither more terrible nor mysterious than any other. Time is the harvester. This is his granary. And as the living pass through, philosophical inscriptions carved in marble and inset into the tunnel walls remind them wryly of the brevity of their journey, the certainty of their common destinations. During the World War II German occupation of Paris, the catacombs served as a headquarters of the Résistance. A congenial base it must have been for that desperate work. For if man's end is inescapable, as those walls of bones affirm, then what matters except the means of getting there—love of country being perhaps as good as any?

We made the trek together through those tunnels one afternoon not long ago, loitering as we went to read the marble wall plaques, admiring the neatness with which all these former citizens had been accommodated. One thing we noticed about the rows and arrangement of skulls was their surprising smallness, considering all the real and imagined worlds a single human mind can contain.

The laying of the first stone of the Cathedral of Notre-Dame, the English usurpation of the French crown, the horror years of the Black Death, the reign of the Sun King, the revolution with its busy *snick-snick* of the guillotine, the coronation of the emperor Napoleon—all that and more was witnessed by the owners of these dry and polished carapaces from which the memories had fled.

"It's funny to think," my daughter said, "that they all had lives. They all had dreams."

Then we mounted another stairway and came up onto a different street, blocks from the place we'd entered. A crowd was gathered on the sidewalk. And on a cool autumn day of this year of our own lives, a young man in a top hat was doing magic with one hand while, with the other, he turned the crank of a wooden music box to send up a happy tune.

57

IN THE HOLLOW HOUR of half past 2 o'clock of the morning before last, an apartment building two blocks from ours blew up.

The sound of it was unmistakable for anything but an explosion. There was no anticipatory crackle, as precedes a near crash of thunder. Nor did it roll sonorously away to silence afterward. The blast was instant and self-contained—of such violence it seemed to heave the floor under our bed. I cannot imagine a bomb landing with greater force. We sprang immediately from sleep and drew back the window curtain. For a moment, all outside was blackness.

Then, over the rooftop of the café on the circle of our street and the roofs and chimney pots beyond, a roseate glow could be seen spreading. Orange flames shot upward through the smoke, speckled with darker objects and fragments being sucked aloft by the tremendous draft. Lights began to flash on in other buildings of the neighborhood. Soon every window was fretted with the heads of residents leaning out to look. Few cars were moving at that hour. Below in the street, groups of people, mostly young, wearing whatever clothes they'd hastily thrown on, came walking and running around the circle to disappear up the small street in the direction of the flames. In the far distance, the *WOOOO-ahh* of sirens began to rise.

There was a time when I would have been down there with the young folks, running toward the center of the excitement. But that was years and years ago, before I had to go to too many fires as a matter of duty and witnessed near at hand what they do to people. Once you have seen how victims crawl into half-filled bathtubs as a last retreat, you never want to attend an apartment fire again.

So I watched from our window as the ladder and pumper trucks arrived, five or six of them, and turned down the street into which the spectators on foot had run. After those, two more trucks came and waited, blue lights revolving, at the entrance to the street, as reinforcements if they were needed. From the erratic behavior of the flames—leaping high into the smoke, subsiding, then bursting up again but less high than before—it appeared the situation was being brought under control. Then no more flames could be noticed at all, only the diminishing glow. And after that you could see the firemen's searchlights playing inquisitively across the faces and slanted roofs of the adjoining buildings.

In Changing Light

The young people came back along the street, slower than they had gone, gesturing with their hands, shoulders bunched up inside their coats now that excitement had given way to the rawness of the hour. No ambulances had been noticed to come or go, and that was encouraging. Windows were being closed along the street. Lights behind them were going out. We went back to bed and to sleep, then. But all through the rest of the night we would come briefly bolt awake at the least sharp noise—the clank of a plumbing pipe, the rattle of a passing truck—anywhere in or near the building.

Yesterday dawned sunny. And though we almost were afraid to know, we walked over to see what had happened.

The crowd was a morning crowd, subdued and analytical. A gas leak had been at fault, either in an apartment on the sixth floor or in the utility space above it. The accumulation must have been considerable. Because the explosion, when it came, shot out through the two sides of the building as from the barrels of a cannon. Structural pieces had been flung into the street in front and the courtyard behind. For a block in both directions, nearly every window pane had been shattered by the concussive force. Crews of men with shovels, carts and trucks were scooping up the glass. You have never seen so much broken glass—tons of it. Already you could hear the *chink-chinking* sound of glaziers at work, putting windows back in the other buildings. People were out on their balconies, sweeping up more glass in dustpans—people who, in that blinding instant of a few hours before, must have imagined they were dead.

Even in the blasted structure there were signs of life. Occupants were carrying out water soaked belongings to hang on terrace railings in the sun. A man and woman, both nicely dressed, were taking photographs.

"That apartment was ours," the man said, pointing to one of the worst-wrecked parts of the building. He snapped another picture of the place he used to live.

"And how about people?" I asked his wife.

"No dead," she said. The occupants on the sixth floor, where the blast had centered, were away on vacation. "And not even any *blessés*—no injured."

Considering the violence of the event, it was almost impossible to believe.

"It is miraculous," she said. Her husband closed his camera back in its case. "Miraculous!" they said again together, with what seemed genuine happiness. And holding hands, walking with the jauntiness of people who know the real meaning of luck, they went off with shoes grinding in the glass to have breakfast at the café on the circle of the street.

58

THE QUESTION OF whether art mirrors life or, just possibly, life imitates art is a pit of controversy into which I don't mean to fall. It's conceivable that neither is the case—that art and life are separate realities, a universe apart. But after living here a while I cannot quite believe that.

Several weeks ago we had a scare. Our friend, Hervé Marc, went off to run in the New York City marathon. A couple of days later we opened the newspaper to a headline that said, "French Marathoner Dies in New York Heat, Humidity." It wasn't Hervé, though. A little past the 18-mile mark, with people dropping all around him, he'd decided he didn't want to die and so had walked part of the rest of the way.

The crowds were wonderful, he said. In Harlem, an enormous black man had given him a piece of ice to apply to the back of his neck. So, in spite of his countryman's misfortune, he remembers New York as a friendly place. Hervé is in his late

20s, the manager of a scientific magazine. The other evening, to celebrate his having come home alive, we went together for dinner at a restaurant he knows, hidden in the recesses of a crooked, cobbled lane near his apartment in the Latin Quarter. It is a place that, without someone to guide you there, you'd likely never stumble on at all.

The restaurant occupied what in the 14th century had been some prosperous burgher's house. It remained divided into a maze of small rooms, with stone walls and door lintels, stained glass in the street windows and dark, hewn-beam ceilings low overhead. After we had eaten, we carried our glasses and followed Hervé down a stone stairway to the establishment's *salon*. There, blissfully filled, the diners all adjourned to have their coffee or whatever else they wanted.

The scene was wonderful. In that small room, sunk down a bit below the level of the street, people were settled in a confusion of soft, deep chairs, some of them half-reclining, vest buttons undone for greater ease. Snatches of unrelated conversations could be heard, some animated, most lazy and contented. Against the ceiling was suspended a blue layer of cigar smoke. At one side, a fire threw out warmth and uneven light from an open hearth.

There was suddenly the oddest sensation—of having stepped not into a room but into a painting. And not just *any* painting, but one by a particular artist. I saw that scene as I imagine Édouard Manet would have rendered it, with that strange, mixed tone of voluptuous formality that he managed somehow to achieve. Now the question is this: Since it may be said with fair probability that everyone in the place would have been familiar with Manet, to what extent might their sense of the moment, of themselves, that scene, their place in it, have been colored by their accidental, even unacknowledged memory of the artist's work?

In short, could an argument be made, however unprovable,

that in that instant, in some unconscious way, life was mirroring art?

A night or two later we had a different but related experience. We had gone in late afternoon to a small museum on the lower side of a park in the far western part of Paris—a house in which hangs the most amazing collection of the paintings of Claude Monet and a few of his contemporaries. Oil colors and canvas cloth, as anyone knows, are dead materials, incapable of generating light or motion. Yet, as we stood in the center of those rooms, there was all about us on the walls a powerful and luminous and animate vitality—an impression of worlds alive, lit by their own suns, and of events ongoing and unfinished.

Leaving there, we came out into the park just at dusk. Children were being ridden on a small carousel, an ancient, iron-spoked, cogged machine, yet so perfectly suspended and balanced that it was being turned by hand by an old woman in a wool coat.

The horses the children sat on were carved of wood and as old as the rest of the carousel. Some had lost an ear. Nearly all had lost their hair-bristle tails. Their paint was faded and their wooden backs were polished from having been ridden so long—a half-century or more, from the look of them and the machine. In no other city I know would one find an apparatus like that still in use. The gears would be motor-driven. The horses would be made of some Space Age polymer, indestructible by time or weather. It would never age. But one day, in favor of some more elaborate novelty, it would be scrapped.

Yet here the old carousel and its tired horses spun in the dusk, the children sitting solemnly aboard, the old woman pushing them around. It was, we thought as we walked on and past, a scene one would not be surprised to see framed on a museum wall. Life may not imitate art deliberately. But Paris does not ever, for a moment, forget it is a painter's city.

59

O<small>N RAINY EVENINGS</small> the slate-gray pigeon takes shelter on the ledge and, tilting his head, looks at us in the light and warmth of our kitchen with a beady, envious eye. The window swings outward on a pivot. There is no screen. Only his respect for the natural order prevents him from joining us inside.

He is fat and fearless, as all this city's pigeons are. No one molests them. They waddle in great numbers along the sidewalks, tamer than barnyard hens and more slothful, moving aside with a show of irritation to let other pedestrians pass. If you were discreet about it, and not too finicky, there would never be any reason to go hungry in Paris.

I rather like the pigeons. So ludicrously awkward afoot, they are transformed by flight. Rising up from the nearly-bare branches of the chestnut trees on the far side of the street, they bank in formation against the faces of the buildings, plane westward across the river and mount until they are a cluster of specks above the hilltop of Saint-Cloud. Then, in an instant, they are back to settle in the leafless trees.

They make these sorties for the pure joy of it, I believe—to prove to themselves and their fellows that they are not just oafish, comic creatures, after all. And they devour the sky with a marvelous ease.

My wife does not care for them, though. Especially she doesn't like the rainy-night one outside the kitchen window. His red eye peering in makes her nervous. She prefers her birds at a distance. Even when you do not see him you can hear him there, grumbling in his throat. He seems dissatisfied with the rules. Someday, I tell her, he is coming in. She doesn't laugh.

Few other birds one sees or hears here.

Just in recent days, a migration of blackbirds has been passing through. If you happen to go out in the still-dark of morning you hear the sleepy chitter of them roosted in the branches. In the daytime they have gone on to wherever it is they're finally headed. And then at sunset the next wave arrives to rest the night.

Quail also migrate south—or some bird the Europeans call by that name. In the newspaper this morning I read how they pass down in vast numbers across the Mediterranean and fall, exhausted, into the nets of Bedouin trappers. American quails are winter-hardy little birds that stand their ground against the season. But this European variety is said to be a delicacy, much favored in the restaurants of Egypt. When the annual passage of the quail is finished, the article said, the Egyptians go back to eating pigeons. I am keeping that bit of intelligence in reserve, to tell the one on our ledge if he gets too cheeky.

There are other sure signs of the turn to winter.

Derelicts—*clochards,* the French call them—are more often seen now on the benches of the underground métro stations late at night, when the last trains are running. They seem to sleep there unbothered by the police. In Paris, as anywhere else, the roofless must have a place.

Café tables are no longer set out on the sidewalk. We take our coffee indoors, behind a steamy glass. People are gray shadows passing in heavy coats.

The thieving bands of Gypsies that prowled quick-handed among the summer tourists have disappeared, flown away to somewhere like the quail—though gaudier, and uncatchable in any net.

On days the sun is out, the Seine still can sparkle like a band of stippled silver. But most times, now, it slides under its bridges as dark and heavy as oil, bending through the city then bearing north and westward to the colder sea. The Tuileries Garden is empty. The domes and towers of monumental public buildings are seen in blue outline, like ships in a fog.

"He's here again!" my wife cries from time to time from the

The Tuileries, autumn

kitchen. And listening, I can hear him there on the ledge, grumbling his winter complaint.

I don't mind pigeons, as I say. But that one has begun to bother me. His patience reminds me that our time is winding down—that we will leave, and he will still be there. I may have to go look him directly in his red eye and remind him of those Egyptians, who, when opportunity presents itself at their window, know what to do with it.

The Winter City

60

Monsieur Wong spied me through the window of the barbershop and stepped inside to visit for a minute beside the chair.

He and his wife own the small Chinese restaurant on our street. Actually there are two Chinese restaurants—a large and prosperous place called Millions of Dragons, and theirs, the little one almost directly across from that, called simply Chez Wong. Though due to a mistake in printing, the card they pass out to customers says Chez *Vong*. It's a humble eatery by Paris standards. But the food is tasty, the prices sensible, and the Wongs, grateful when someone comes in their door, are touchingly attentive. We went there several times in the first weeks, and have been meaning to go again. Monsieur Wong never fails to stop and pass a word or two if he sees us taking our afternoon coffee in a café.

He and his wife are not yet 40, too young to be defeated. But this day his face was long. Business was slow, he said—very slow. If you have a restaurant of a dozen tables and no one comes to sit at them, you have a major problem. He did not know what the matter was. It was not yet the holidays. The city was full of people. They must eat somewhere.

"The problem," the barber told him, "is who wants to eat the *cuisine chinoise?* This is Paris. People want the good *cuisine française.*"

"Perhaps," Monsieur Wong said sadly. "But I see them go in and out across the street." I reached out from under the barber's sheet to shake his hand as he left. Probably business would improve, I said. I promised to come again soon and bring my family.

"You ought to have a good French restaurant," the barber told him.

"Yes," said Monsieur Wong. "But I am Chinese." And he went off to fold his napkins and start his kettles boiling.

At every hand one is struck by the sense of small lives precariously balanced. And for many of those the margin is even finer than Monsieur Wong's.

We have another friend—call him Oumar, so as not to risk aggravating his difficulty. Oumar has a job which pays him 4,000 francs a month, the equivalent of a bit more than $400. He lives sparely, has no expensive habits and few indulgences. And that sum would suffice, were it not for his unreasonable generosity. Some acquaintance needs 1,000 francs to meet a sudden emergency. Oumar asks himself, *What are friends for?* Without hesitation, the money is drawn out of the bank. A woman he knows, an immigrant from Warsaw, has gone in partnership with another woman to start a tiny Polish café. But for the venture to succeed, she had to have an espresso coffee machine. So of course she went to Oumar. The amount she required was great, 5,000 francs. But how could he refuse? Shouldn't she have a chance to make a life? So he visited the bank again.

He took me the other day to see her place. The coffee machine, large and chrome-plated, sparkled on the counter. But the other woman, the partner, had turned out to be useless. She sat behind the bar, eating chocolate and drinking endless cups of coffee from the splendid new machine. The work, when there was any, fell entirely to Oumar's friend. The café had six tables and five stools, but except for us there was no one in the place. And I could have told him, if he had not guessed it already, that he had little prospect of getting his money back.

Lately his affairs took a serious turn. The police notified his employer that unless Oumar got a work permit he would have to be discharged. He had tried before to get the permit. But for someone who is non-French, with his few skills and especially from his part of the world, it is a document almost impossible to obtain.

Last month he went by train to a city in eastern France, where he has friends. The friends had located a young woman who would marry him if he paid her 9,000 francs. He gave her the money and a civil ceremony was performed. He also gave her a ticket to come to Paris at her first convenience and appear with him before the police, so that he might get his work permit. Now Oumar waits. But she does not come. When he telephones to that other city, she can never be located. It seems she has always just gone out. He begins to suspect that she has cashed the ticket and spent the money, and that he has seen the last both of his 9,000 francs and of this wife he knows only by her name printed on the certificate of marriage.

I wonder sometimes what the future holds for him—what it holds for any of these little people, and the thousands more whose stories resemble theirs, who live on the crumbling edge.

Last night we went out to eat. Our consciences told us it should have been to Chez Wong, but the desperate hospitality there and the emptiness of those other tables are too disheartening. We walked the opposite way along the street, instead, to a plain but cheerful Romanian place we know, full of a lively company of East Europeans, with recorded violin music and wine flowing and a racket of voices competing to be heard.

61

I SAW HER FIRST across a room, among some other people. Her presence attracted and overcame me in a way that now, even days later, I scarcely can describe. It must be the sort of thing that can happen to a man of a certain age anywhere, in any city, although it may happen more often here.

The other people in the room, a dozen or so of them, were caught up in lively conversation, but she stood a bit to the side and took no part in that. So I was able to study her covertly for several minutes from just inside the doorway.

How young she was I couldn't say. So many other things I noticed first. To begin with, her soft-brimmed straw hat was ridiculously out of season. Pale winter light fell in slanting rays through the tall windows of the house. Outside, below and behind her, was the garden, its lawn littered with crisp leaves, the flowers finished. Yet there she was, quite unconcerned, pleased to have on her summer straw with its satin ribbon and a bunch of rosebuds fastened at the front.

Her hair, too, was out of style—part of it gathered up under the hat, the rest falling to her shoulders in soft cascades, longer than one usually sees it worn in Paris nowadays. About her dress I can't say much except that its collar was open at the throat, and around her shoulders she had knotted a kind of light shawl.

But all this—hat, hair, collar and shawl—was only decoration to frame her face. Halted there where I'd entered the room, I tried not to be too rude or obvious about it. But I could not make my eyes leave her. What struck me about that face was its play of contradictions—at once childish and womanly, expectant and knowing, a bit indulgent yet forceful, refined without being weak. Her eyes under distinct, natural brows were large, astonishingly dark and deep. Her nose, by no means aristocratic, turned up in a suggestion of a pug. As she looked at the others in the room and listened to what they said, her lips were parted slightly in interest or amusement.

How to explain, exactly, how I was affected?

It wasn't merely that she was the most beautiful young woman I'd ever seen. It was more complicated than that. There was, in her, something of my daughters' freshness, though they still are several years younger. And also a sense, reassembled out of sudden memory, of all the passions and devotions of a far distant time in one's own life, and of all the loveliness ever seen since in all the years, though briefly and at a distance.

Looking secretly at the others, I was amazed to see that evidently they were not smitten by her in the same way I had been. They talked a while, then moved on into the next room. And the two of us were left alone for a moment.

Coming closer, I could see how she'd been fashioned. The dark eyes into which I'd fallen were, after all, only holes torn carelessly in the clay. The faint marks of the shaping tool still could be seen on the lustrous curve of her cheek. The house with its tall windows and its garden full of winter light had been the home and workshop of the sculptor, Auguste Rodin. And it was hard to imagine that those hands, inclined to shaping forms of strength and mass and restless movement, had ever paused to make so delicate a thing as her. Her name was simply *Girl With a Flowered Hat*—she hadn't any other. And she was more than 100 years old.

Yet, knowing all this, I stepped just a little back from her and looked again. And again she took my heart away.

I spoke of this afterward to my wife—it seemed a safe enough infidelity to report—and to an artist friend with whom we spent part of the day. But our friend had not much regard for her. He preferred Rodin's monumental works in bronze, *The Thinker, The Burghers of Calais,* the impressionistic statue of Balzac standing in the garden outside.

Girl With a Flowered Hat

PHOTOGRAPH BY BRUNO JARRET, COURTESY OF THE MUSÉE RODIN, PARIS

"She's pretty," he said. "But I'm not much into *prettiness*."

He seemed to me afflicted with an awful blindness. But there was no use to argue. The two of us would never see her with the same eye. That's how it is with love at any age.

62

OUR NEW FRIENDS, Guy and Katherine, live on the river. Not *beside* the river, or *near* the river, or any other such approximation. They actually live upon it, its current sliding eternally under them as they plan and dream. Guy is 40 years old, a tiny, impish man with an ungovernably reckless nature. He is a documentary film-maker by profession. Katherine is a long and tawny lady, several years younger and a full head taller, who, though she projects a quiet strength, is amused by Guy and indulgent of his wild inspirations, of which the chief one is the house itself.

Guy admits to having been ruled for a long time by two desires. The first was to build, with his own hands, a home for his family. The other was to have a country house in Paris. Three years ago he found a derelict barge tethered 28 miles downstream on the Seine. Where lesser men might only have seen rust and trouble, he saw a grand design unfolding in his mind.

He bought the thing. The wheelhouse on the rear deck was intact and, under it, the barge master's quarters as well, a wood-paneled cabin six steps square. The oldest of their four children was 13 then, the youngest only two months. For two winters and a summer that cabin was their home, though in fair weather a tent pitched on the deck above served as an annex. The rest, 125 feet long in all, was only the open iron hull in which cargoes of wheat and coal and sand had been freighted to and from the heart of France.

After many bureaucratic adventures, moorage finally was arranged. By some miracle the ancient engine started. It took nine hours to make the 28 miles against the river's flow. Then Guy nosed his barge against the bank, just above the bridge two blocks west of our traffic circle. He ran water to it, and an electric line. And he began to build.

Handiness with tools? He hadn't any. Plumbing, wiring, carpentry, the welder's trade—he had to learn it all. First he floored the open hull, then raised a roof over that. He used a plumb line to be sure his walls were true, then found that a drop in the river had caused his barge to list, so that when it righted the whole superstructure leaned. He tore it down and built again.

Meter by meter he has expanded their domain, his working clutter receding toward either end as he advances. Every time we are there, it seems, another wall has gone up, another hall or room has been created. Now Katherine has a modern kitchen, with a dishwasher. The children all have bedrooms, with the barge master's stateroom kept for guests. There is a vast dining area, and a studio where Guy can work at editing film. Soon, on the lower level, there will be an enormous *salon*—a living room with fireplace. When Guy is finished, his home afloat will be almost unimaginably spacious by the standards of this apartment city. And it will be—indeed, it already is—a country house. Great trees on the embankment shade it. And on a strip of fertile soil beside their boat, he and Katherine this year grew flowers and vegetables, the sort of garden a proper country house should have.

They invited us for dinner one night not long ago. Katherine carried to the table steaming bowls of mussels and cockles, and after that a plate of veal and mushrooms. The wine was dry and sharp. Barge tows ploughed up and down the Seine just outside the windows Guy has cut and framed. His boat gave little shudders—*wanting to go with them,* he said—and the hanging lamp over the table swung gently from side to side. Talk ran far into the night, as shipboard conversations are apt to, and a real friendship was cemented.

Soon after that we went together to the sheds of a *brocanteur* they know, a dealer in junk and treasures. Guy and Katherine have prowled there often during their house-making, eyes keen for the odd cabinet or chest whose fine old wood might be liberated from layers of cracked paint. This day Katherine had found two antique ceramic bricks to be heated beside the promised fireplace and put under the covers to warm the foot of the bed. Then Guy came bounding between the towering stacks of gathered stuff, demanding that we must all see what *he* had found. He led us to it.

Two workmen helped lift down a heavy table so the prize could be better seen. "It's from a church," said Guy, and threw back the hinged front. It was an organ, with ivory keys and stops, powered by a foot-treadle bellows.

"It's done!" he cried. "I have bought it. I always wanted an organ. They will bring it with a truck to my boat tomorrow." Katherine was wonderfully expressionless.

"Do you even know how to play the organ?" we asked him.

"No," Guy said happily. "But what difference does it make? The first thing is to find a good wife. After that, it is possible to learn anything."

63

VIOLENCE IS BELIEVED to be less common here than in other cities of comparable size. I have seen no statistics, and so cannot report that for a fact. But it is the generally-held conviction.

You may very well get your pocket picked in the crush of the rush-hour métro train. But it is unlikely that anyone will push you off the platform and under the wheels for the pure amusement of it. An attractive young woman alone may be annoyed by the unceasing overtures of lonely North African men who course the streets in tireless quest of female comfort. But it is more a nuisance than a threat. She is not apt to be dragged into some alleyway and violated. As anywhere, there are districts where it is not recommended to do too much solitary wandering in the deep of night. Gather millions of people together in one place and you will find, among them, a certain irreducible quotient of craziness. As a rule, though, streets here are not a war zone and parks still are for walking or sitting in at almost any reasonable hour.

However, Paris in recent weeks has been agitated by a series of monstrous crimes.

The murders—nine of them, so far, in the past two months—all have occurred in the same part of the city, an area of narrow, twisting streets mounting the butte of Montmartre toward the church of Sacré-Coeur and then spilling down the hill's back side to the northern edge of the city.

Because these predations have been limited to one quarter of Paris, the 18th arrondissement, the murderer—assuming it's the work of a single beast—has been dubbed by the press simply as The Killer of the Eighteenth. His victims, women in their 70s living alone in small apartments, are found throttled or with their skulls broken. Robbery is not clearly the motive. There have been no witnesses. The police are without clues.

The Montmartre district, which through the last century and several years into this one was the center of artistic and intellectual bohemian life, has since suffered a seedy decline. Much antique charm still can be found there, but only if one is willing to run a gauntlet of sex shops and peep shows to seek it out. It also is a district of Paris where pensioners and others of limited means still can afford to live. There are said to be more elderly people quartered there than in any other arrondissement of the city—35,000 of them, by one census. The viciousness in their neighborhood has these older folks angry and alarmed.

Opposition politicians have tried to turn the affair to advantage, implying that you can never know what depravity may be loosed when Socialists come to power—a proposition that is hard to fathom unless President Mitterand and his ministers have taken suddenly to roaming Montmartre with silk stockings over their faces. The government replies that there is crime in every time—an assertion which, though plainly true, does not comfort aged ladies listening for footfalls outside their apartment doors.

The press of Paris is vigorous and varied. There are sober and responsible newspapers, and there are outrageously sensational ones. Journals of the latter kind have been whipped to a veritable frenzy of enterprise by these murders.

One of them conducted a survey in which readers were invited to rank their level of terror by arrondissement. I did not see the published result, but it may safely be guessed that the 18th came high on the list. Another, a couple of days ago, printed a composite drawing of The Killer of the Eighteenth—one of those portraits pasted up from sample books of noses, eyebrows, ears and so forth, which never fail to excite horror precisely because, like Frankenstein's monster, they so obviously are stitched together from borrowed parts.

There turned out to be no basis for the drawing. The paper had concocted it from nothing, as a circulation builder.

But the next day, in a saloon, a young man was drinking a

glass of wine and wondering why everyone in the place was staring at him so strangely. Shortly after that the law arrived. And the young man spent the next 10 hours stripped naked in a police station, trying to explain why someone with a face like that *wouldn't* strangle widows in their sleep.

Two months in which only nine murders were recorded would, for certain urban neighborhoods of this planet, be an interval of almost halcyon civility. But here, where it is not yet taken for granted that people will fall savagely on their fellows as a matter of daily routine, crimes like those being reported from the north of Paris still inspire the florid inventiveness of the popular press.

64

IT HAPPENED we had stepped into the same doorway of a café on the Place Saint-Michel to find a minute's shelter from the beating rain. We stood there under the recess of the eave, two middle-aged men with coats wet nearly through and water running in trickles out of our beards. It turned out we spoke a common tongue, although with different inflections. And on the basis of all these miraculous commonalities, he suggested we take a table inside the place.

In the Latin Quarter you have to watch yourself. It's a fine and interesting part of the city, but almost any sort of eccentricity can be found wandering there. This fellow didn't seem too peculiar, though. Cold and wet, as I was, and maybe a little down on his luck—but not dangerous. Anyway, there's not much trouble you can get into sitting at a café table at half past noon on a rainy Thursday.

"I've just come from giving private English lessons to some

Japanese," he said. "So for the moment I have some money. I'll buy the coffee."

"Never mind," I said. "Let me get it."

"In that case," he told the waiter, "I'll take a beer. The *big* beer."

"*La grande?*" the waiter said.

"Roight! The big one." You could see, when it came, why the waiter wanted to be sure. The mug was bigger than a flower pot and must have held two liters. "Lookit it!" he cried happily. "I can hardly lift the thing." Although, above his beard, he had those blown cheek veins the English seem to get from practice at that kind of lifting.

He was a writer, he said. He'd gotten out of Cambridge University almost 20 years ago and come to Paris, taken a night job in a hotel and begun to write. He'd filled up books with notes. Then he'd run out of money and gone home to take a job as a life-saver on a Cornwall beach—"where the waves come in as high as bloody houses." He saved enough at that to rent a cottage and write some more. The notes he'd made in Paris he organized into a novel, and a publisher bought it straight off.

"It was a big success," he said. "I gave out interviews and had my picture in the papers—all that kind of thing. And I thought, man, this is easy. So I wrote another one, and it was a complete failure. For a while, then, I took what I could get—doing some publicity, teaching a bit. Like that."

I offered him a cigarette.

"I think I have some," he said, and felt his pockets. "Or I'll get some. Or—oh, what the hell. Yes, I'll take one, thanks. But let's get one thing straight," he said. "I'm no bum. I've got money." He took a couple of bills from his pocket to show.

Then he lit the smoke. He was making small inroads on his vat of beer.

"One year I went up to the Edinburgh drama festival," he said, "and I got invited to write a play. Adapted it from a book—not my book, some other fellow's. Surprised hell out of me. People liked it. Good reviews. So I was up again. But after the play there wasn't anything for a while. Then I met my wife—she's American—and I wrote a book of poetry. And what would you know? Another bloody big success."

"And after the poetry book?" I asked him.

"Nothing," he said. "Not a line in print."

"How long's that been?"

"Fourteen years," he said. He said that he and his American wife had come back to Paris, hoping he would write something again. They were living in a hotel a couple of blocks down the quay. He was a good talker, and told all this better and more interestingly than I tell it here. You enjoyed listening to it.

But I looked at my watch. I had an appointment I had to keep.

"Look," he said, "maybe you'd like to get together sometime and talk about writing."

Sure, I told him. Sometime.

"When?" he wanted to know.

I explained I was behind on my newspaper work. And after that I had to make a trip. He didn't know the telephone number at his hotel, so I gave him mine. Next month would be clear, I said. Why didn't he give me a call sometime next month?

"Next *month?*" His face fell. "I was hoping maybe next week. I was going to ask you—" It was a hard thing for him to get out. "I was going to ask if maybe you could let me have a hundred francs until next Thursday."

"Sorry," I told him, maybe sounding even shorter than I meant to.

"Well, of course," he said, "you're *absolutely roight.* I just wanted to see what you'd say. There's nothing worse than a question of money between friends. Well, between acquaintances, at any rate."

I had to go to my appointment. "Sorry," I told him again—halfway meaning it.

184

"It's all right," he said. "Although if you wouldn't mind you might leave me a few cigarettes." When I went out it was still raining, and he was staring out through the wet glass, his face expressionless, most of that enormous beer still undrunk before him.

Late that same evening the phone at our apartment rang. There was a woman on the line. She was the wife, she said, of the man I'd met at the café earlier in the day. He wasn't feeling well, she said. He'd sold blood that afternoon to help cover their bill at the hotel. But he'd given her the telephone number and said she was supposed to call me. She didn't know what about—that was just what he had said.

He must have misunderstood, I told her.

He may have, she said. He was feeling pretty bad. But finally he'd been able to sleep.

65

SUPPOSE THAT YOU began each day on a crowded train platform, waiting to hurl yourself into a still more crowded coach, a coach designed for 24 to sit and 133 to stand. Rarely would you find a seat. Instead, you would be supported and squeezed by the pressing bodies of strangers, the washed and the unwashed, all compacted there like sheep in a pen.

Eventually the train would discharge you up a stair onto the rush-hour sidewalk where, further bumped and jostled, you would make your way through the hurrying throng to your place of work, which might be a desk in some cramped office of little privacy or the counter of a store where more crowds seethed and shouldered.

At day's end, when you were tired, the process would have to be repeated in reverse. Until finally you arrived back at your flat—an apartment that, Paris lodging costing what it does, might well be smaller than suited your own and your family's needs. There, still in close company, you would await another day, another train.

When people live in such numbers and so near, space becomes an issue. And since physical space is unattainable, some other kind of distance must be contrived. That, I believe, explains the manner of Parisians, which so easily is mistaken for sullenness or even hostility. People draw around themselves circles of emotional privacy which others are not permitted to breach. It is their single refuge, out of which they look at the world with faces blank as masks. Hostile it is not, though; only the proof of that basic human need to have, sometimes, a place alone, entirely to oneself, even if it is only in the mind.

Then, with surprising suddenness, the barrier can fall.

On a train at rush hour the other day we watched a blind woman get aboard. She made her way along the platform, white cane pecking the pavement ahead of her, sending messages to the eye of her mind. All the people crowding on the platform gave ground to let her pass. Those already on the coach made way for her to board.

I can think of no surer definition of courage than to travel the métro system of this city sightless—the millions of footfalls thundering along the maze of tunnels, the trains coming and leaving with a rush, the platform's edge giving way without warning to a chasm from which, if you happen to step off into it, there is apt to be no return. Very brave and composed this woman went about her journey, cane showing her the step up into the train, where she counted off the stops. What millions of sighted tourists here are too timid even to attempt, she was doing routinely in the sightless dark.

But boarding and riding are problems of one order. Making the next connection is another. The train halted; its doors slid open. She stepped down and out, and stood a moment on the platform, cane poised, the crowds parting to flow around her. Then a woman stopped. Then another. It was a connecting station, with many intersecting lines, one of which she had to find. From that platform several tunnels led away. The people turned, came back, spoke to her, gently took her arm. Their masks dropped away. They were wonderfully tender in their concern.

Maybe I make too much of this small incident. It was not so remarkable, after all—except that the kindness was done by riders whose faces, only a moment before, had been frozen in expressions that warned the world to keep away. Living too close, too long, can be punishing. In the daily habit of compacted lives, scowls become fixed, the circles of privacy all but impenetrable.

Then came that sightless woman, cane tapping, inhabiting her own vast world of darkness at unimaginable distance from their own. Possibly they sensed in her the ultimate, terrifying possibilities of privacy. Because across that gulf their willing hands reached out. Only for a moment, though—only until the small decency was done. Then, masked and unreachable again, they plunged on with the crowded, lonely marches of their day.

66

WHEN TWILIGHT DEEPENS and pigeons go to roost and the mingled smells of cooking begin to fill the landing of the stair, the night's theater begins in the windows of the building across the street.

I am not, by instinct, a peeping Tom, having always thought there must be more to life than can be seen through a keyhole.

But when I sit to work, I'd rather face a window than a wall. And if the people who live in the apartments directly facing ours insist on keeping their curtains open, the chances are that I will oblige them by sooner or later looking in.

Directly in front, now—stage center, you might say—the red-haired woman has just come home from work. She lives by herself. Each evening at the same hour a light in the sitting room announces her arrival. She reads the mail, if there is any, then may sit to look at a magazine. She is a woman of early middle age, and I have never noticed her to have visitors. Usually it is late before her kitchen light comes on, and then only for a little while as she makes and eats her solitary supper. Then she may go back to read some more. Then all her lights go out. Tonight, though, she has thrown off her coat and gone directly to the kitchen, where she can be seen drawing water into pans, taking down boxes from the cupboard—moving quickly, purposefully, as if inspired.

Below and to the left is the Arab family. Only a man and wife, actually. They seem to have no children. He goes away in the morning and, afterward, it used to be her habit to stand long hours at the open window, arms folded on the ledge, staring out into the alien city. Once, this past summer, when my own family had gone out and I was daydreaming from my window in exactly the same way, I impulsively waved to her across the 50 yards or so that separated us, surely a safe enough distance for a greeting, even from a total stranger. My trespass alarmed her, though. For many days she did not come to her window again. And even now, in winter, when she is working behind the closed glass at night, it seems to me that she is careful never to turn her face this way.

On the top floor, the 10th, are the people whose white cat, in fair weather, used to take his exercise on the slim perch of the outer ledge. Sharing the cat's space—inside, not on the ledge—are an older woman and a boy and girl who appear to be not much past 20.

It is impossible to guess whether the woman is raising her family alone, or whether the younger two are married and she is the resident mother of one of them. She busies herself all day around the apartment, cleaning, laundering, cooking. The young ones are kept fully occupied with vanity. Each night, before retiring, the girl spends a half-hour at a minimum brushing her dark hair. Probably she counts the strokes aloud for all to hear. The boy is a body builder. After exercising, he strikes muscular poses in front of a mirror to inspect the result.

To the right of them lives a rather portly man whose shower faces directly on the street, although he seems indifferent to this regrettable arrangement. The window has no curtain. He bathes often and meticulously working up a terrific lather, then using various long-handled implements to get at the unreachable parts of his back. I don't know what filth he is trying to wash away, but surely it must be nearly gone by now. He may be the cleanest human being in the Western world. Each night he works at this until steam from the shower clouds the glass.

Four floors directly underneath is another man, an old man, whose daily uniform is a gray knitted sweater. He moves with a pained and shuffling step, and sits at a small table to take his meals alone. His life appears to be a joyless succession of long silences.

A bit above him, and to the right, is a woman of his same age, white-haired, also alone and wrapped in a silence just as great. I find myself wondering if they have ever met, those two, in the elevator or on their difficult ascents of the stair. Or if they ever will. And, if they should, what possibly might come of it.

And so it goes: Several dozen windows facing, and inside each of those a playlet proceeding—small dramas into which one finds oneself finally drawn, in spite of any scruples about peeping.

For example, several moments ago the red-haired woman

came back into her kitchen. She had changed from her dull working clothes into a bright green dress, which I must say suited her very nicely. What's more, there was a gentleman with her. So tonight, as the song goes . . . *tonight is not just any night.* She is laughing and animated. Together they look into the pots on the stove. Now he has opened a bottle of wine and she has poured their glasses full.

How does the play end for her? For any of them? We will not be here to know.

67

At the intersection of our street, where bicyclists, motor-cyclists and folks afoot seem to get so regularly felled, I witnessed the other morning a most extraordinary spectacle of conflict. What it means, exactly, I can't say—unless it is that civilization just may triumph over machines, after all. Provided, that is, that civilization stands its ground.

I was headed off at an early hour to see if by some stroke of luck, by connivance and wheedling and saintly patience, I could manage to get some of my own money out of the bank, never a simple transaction here. French banks accept your money gladly, but dole it back out only with great suspicion.

At the intersection, a man was crossing with the pedestrian signal toward the far side of the street. He was an old man, in his 70s, I suppose, slight of stature, with a shock of unruly white hair, but very straight and dignified in his striped blue suit. With one hand he leaned heavily on a cane. In the other hand he carried his long morning loaf. Looking neither right nor left, he made his way out into the crosswalk, as the signal entitled him to do.

An enormous cement-mixer truck, vat revolving slowly on its back, was turning at the corner. It had advanced exactly to the crosswalk and had braked there, waiting for the way to clear. But evidently the man with the cane did not proceed quickly enough to suit the driver, who gave a honk on the truck's horn. The little man stopped stock-still in his tracks. With vast, grave dignity he turned and looked up over the huge grill at the driver, seated high behind the windshield. Pointing up there with the end of his loaf, the man on foot commenced a short lecture on the manners of the street.

A comic tableau, it was: that single slight figure, lame with years, giving not one inch of quarter to the iron thing hulking over him, weighing multiples of tons. Having said his piece, the old man turned to continue on his way. Then the truck driver made a mistake. He honked again.

The small man froze in mid-step. He turned with disbelief. He cried something in a voice of trembling outrage. And the driver, doggedly provocative, honked back. That last one was one honk too many. The old man began to lay on with his cane. He beat the truck over the fender, then across its grill, then moved a couple of steps to get a better angle for lashing at the other fender. The iron carcass of the machine did not yield; it was made of durable stuff. But the clatter of wood against metal chimed loudly along the street. Other passers-by stopped and turned to watch. Until finally, with an especially well-struck blow, the cane shattered and the end of it spun off to lodge against the curb.

The small man drew himself up, then, brushed back his white hair and, panting slightly from his exertions, continued his march to the far side of the street. The truck driver, a youngish fellow, had peered down at these sudden violences with a startled look. Trucks now and then run over people, you could almost see him thinking, *but people oughtn't to run over trucks.* That violated his notion of propriety. And so, determined to have the last word, he gave a parting honk.

Just a small honk, it was. But, whirling around, the old man started back into the street, brandishing his bread loaf and what was left of his cane—only the handle and splintered stump—plainly ready and eager to see the matter through to some final result. Whereupon the driver slumped down meekly in his seat, engaged the truck's gears and, without issuing any further challenges, got on out of there while the getting was good.

No cheers went up from those of us who had observed this confrontation. But from the smiles of amusement and satisfaction, you could tell that none of us had been on the side of the truck. I went ahead to the bank, then. And encountered there the usual difficulty. It seemed the computer was acting up. Maybe if I came back in the afternoon, the clerk said, I could make a withdrawal. *Nothing doing,* I said—drawing myself up as straight as that little man with the cane. "The computer is *your* problem," I told him. "The money belongs to me."

And I stood there until the cash was counted out.

68

THE OPEN-AIR MARKET appeared again this morning, stretching the whole length of the block and drawing a great crowd of customers from the quarter.

These surprising manifestations are not, we now know, random and magical. Logic governs them—a logic that simply passed undetected during the laze and drift of the sweet, uncounted summer and autumn days. In fact, the market comes once monthly to this street. And under the tent canopies of the stalls, the produce tells the passage of the year.

The choice today was of end-of-season country things.

From the market, Route de la Reine

Plump, irregular loaves of brown wheat bread, burnt at the edges and dusty from the oven; gold-dripping slabs of honeycomb directly out of the farmer's hive; geese, come fat a shade too early for Christmas, hung naked by their necks in startled rows; enormous orange pumpkins, some big around as bushels, sold here not whole but by the slice; cases of the new Beaujolais, brought in by small vintners; cheeses by the wheel or the wedge; late cabbages and celery roots for shredding; jars of kitchen jellies pressed from the last fruit of the branch and offered by farm women in head-scarves; dried flowers and tart little skillet-fried pies, stuffed with slices of knobby, late-ripening apples . . .

And under the awning on the sidewalk in front of the brasserie Le Narval, where the tables of the coffee-drinkers used to be, a fishmonger was selling cockles, mussels and oysters from the shore of the cold Breton sea. Overnight, all that materialized along the block of our street—the vendors calling out for notice of their goods, the crowds shouldering by with satchels and two-wheeled pull carts, stepping around a tiny mottled she-goat with a week-old kid no bigger than a kitten.

Our neighbor, the widow of the symphony conductor, has a sense of history. And she tells about it in a voice so far from the hasty argot, in language so refined and precise, that even the inexpert ear can perfectly understand. The street running by here is called the Route de la Reine—the way of the queen—because, she says, in royal times the queens of France used to pass along it on their way to pleasure in their châteaux beyond the river to the west.

One imagines that as it must have been. The unpaved road pooled with rain in this season, or maybe crusted with frost; the horses leaning hard forward in their harnesses, blowing steam, hooves slipping and throwing up gouts of mud; the ornate carriages lurching in the ruts. Perhaps there would have been a market here then. Or, if not exactly here, then somewhere along that route. The party of servants riding horseback or in wagons behind might well have halted to look quickly through the stalls for something to surprise and please her majesty's taste. The vendors' cries would be suddenly subdued and the peasant crowd would crane necks to see if, in the lifting of a curtain at a carriage window, a glimpse of God's splendor on Earth might be revealed. Then the procession would move grandly on the several hundred yards to the Seine, traversing the wide, dark flow by some means not evident now—though surely either by barge or wooden bridge—and finally, in all its magnificence, would pass into the far trees and out of view.

The way of the queens is paved now, of course, with signals winking and cars rushing along it at nearly every hour in a raucous stream. Buildings press in from either side, where wood and meadow used to be. A steel bridge has taken all hazard or mystery from the river crossing. Yet on these occasional days when we walk outside and find a country market sprouted and noisily thriving, the history of which our neighbor tells is easier imagined.

Today we filled our bags with tasty things, passing up the goat and the long-necked geese, and brought back fried pies to eat instead of lunch. As afternoon drew on, raw wind began whipping at the tents of the stalls. Then, almost as suddenly as revolution disposed of kings and queens, a winter rain came to wash market and people away.

69

THE FRENCH high-speed rail service is a miracle of comfort and convenience. Hurtling at speeds of more than 150 miles an hour on the newest sections of track, the *Train à Grande Vitesse,* or TGV, brings the sunny Mediterranean only five and a fraction hours away from Paris, or Geneva and the snow of the Alps a mere three and one-half hours. Meals with wine, ordered when the ticket is booked, are brought on trays to riders in the first-class coaches. Silently the train devours the distances, while for the passengers, settled in their reclining seats, speed is noticeable only in the way fields and villages slide past the window in a fluid blur.

Thousands of people ride the TGV each day and take these wonders for granted. But to fully appreciate the miracle, it is necessary to arrive at the station three minutes after the train has left, as is fairly probable if your departure is at an early hour and you are traveling in the company of two daughters and one wife. The technology of hot curlers and hair blowers has not kept pace with advances in modern railroading. And French trains go on time.

Our ticket entitled us to ride the TGV southeast to Aix-les-Bains. From there, after a bit of a wait, a regular train would deliver us through a mountain tunnel directly into the Fréjus valley of Italy, arriving at the ski village of Bardonecchia in time for lunch.

But a ticket must never be thought of as a fixed plan of events as they will actually unfold. A ticket is only an expression of general intent, a theoretical instrument. Come panting with your holiday baggage and your beautifully-coiffed ladies an hour before dawn onto a platform from which the train has just gone and you discover the emptiness of theory. As if by magic, a simple half-day journey was transformed into a pilgrimage.

At mid-morning there was another train, a slow one—five hours to Lyon, enjoying conversation with other riders in a shared compartment, stopping wherever a station sign, a flock of geese and the smoke from a few chimneys announced the possibility of life. From Lyon the way lay due east on a different train, older still and slower, with straight-backed seats. Two hours, I understood the agent to say it was, until the next change at the town of Chambéry.

We dozed. An hour passed. The train stopped and I woke and stretched, then wandered idly outside the coach to see what place this was we'd reached. CHAMBÉRY, the sign said.

With a thin screech of panic I leapt back aboard. And dragging down our duffel from the overhead racks we stumbled along the aisle of the car, our daughters close behind, and out onto the platform. We congratulated ourselves on our luck, my wife and I. The train began slowly to pull away. Then we looked behind us for the girls. Except for one other man, the platform was empty. They'd gotten stuck in the door; then the door had locked. They were still aboard, bound for somewhere. I ran along the platform beside the train, which was gathering speed.

"Mes enfants!" I was shouting. My children!

"A pity," the man said as I ran past. "It's gone." They can be wonderfully sympathetic, the French.

The engineer, when I caught up with him, looked down amazed at the weathered but nimble apparition bounding along beneath his locomotive window—startled as a pilot might be who'd just seen an angel outside the cockpit at 30,000 feet.

"Mes enfants!" I screamed up at him. He stopped the train.

We ate candy bars and drank coffee and chocolate from a machine, pleased as anything to be all together. While wrenching at the locked train door, the girls said afterward, a future as nomadic orphans had passed before their eyes.

The next train, the third, was full of skiers and school children, bound at dusk for the French border town of Modane. Laboring, it climbed and wound among the darkening peaks. Wind whistled at the window cracks. The seats were hard, the car cold and stifling by fits. Full night closed down.

In the little station café at Modane, two French customs officials and two Italian ones were taking their coffees together.

The train from there was some relic of the war they'd all forgotten—an armored locomotive and four coaches, painted military green. A cone of light shone down from a single hooded bulb on the platform. A bicycle was chained to the light post, waiting for some ghost in long green coat and helmet to mount it and pedal away with rifle slung. I climbed up the ladder on the side of the engine and knocked on the lighted window, and the engineer opened it to say, yes, it was the train to Bardonecchia, the last one of the night. He let us on board with two other passengers and a woman conductor. And giving a high, reedy pipe on his engine's whistle, drew us through the several miles of tunnel into that village, where white-flanked mountains towered around and the night air smelled of horses and frost and chocolate and cooking pasta. And thus, a little before bedtime, we were delivered to our lodging and to our friends, who had not missed the morning's early train from Paris and had begun to wonder if we were coming, after all.

That's the hectic way we went.

Our return was a model of regularity. Two hours early to the station. One train straight through to Chambéry, connecting with the *Grande Vitesse* direct to Paris. And it is a marvel, the fast train. The seats are deep and well cushioned. Smooth as a rush of wind, banking like an airplane on the turns, it flies across the country in an orange streak.

It saves a lot of time, if saving time is the most important part of travel. You get on, babies cry a while, and in hardly any time, having covered a prodigious distance, you get off. But beyond that, come to think of it, there's little to remember and less to tell.

70

I HAVE ALWAYS HATED ENDINGS, and most of all the way things start to end before they are really finished. The way, for example, that a book sometimes transports you far outside yourself—but then the last is spoiled by the sadness of pages growing thin between your fingers. Or the way a vacation place takes on an air of unreality in the final days, the clarity of sky and water receding, the shore sounds strangely muted, as if suddenly seen and heard from greater distance.

My mother hated endings. She raged against them inside herself until she physically sickened. We dislike them, too, and have made a rule of never speaking of them, of never counting days. And yet it has happened here.

Looking from the window toward the river and the hill of Saint-Cloud beyond, its forest skeletal and brown now that a night of driving wind has carried the last of the leaves away, I see a panorama—rooftops, chimneys, steeple—of which strangely I feel less a part. Even between us and friends here I sense a certain distance growing. All that we will ever know of one another we know already. There is little time for further investments.

Our neighbor on the landing, Georges Farchakh, came back not long ago from another trip to his native Lebanon. This time he'd been gone a month. He brought us a package of Lebanese sweets, cookies with fillings at their center, and sat to drink a tea. Things had seemed better to him there, he said. A *little* better—and he held one thumb and forefinger a fraction apart to show how small the gain had been. Still, he said, if the Israelis go, and after the Israelis the Syrians, and if some means can be found to keep the peace, and if the Americans do no more half-hearted dabbling . . . if all these miracles transpire, then it is just possible the fragile civility of Lebanon might be reconstructed.

199

Georges' wife, Salma, we have learned, is Syrian. He a Lebanese Christian, she a Moslem. They met in younger years here in Paris, before his country was the occupied, hers one of the occupiers. Seeing them together, with their daughter, one realizes how little, in the larger scheme, sectarian dogmas and raging nationalism count for.

No sooner had Georges returned than Salma had to leave. She is an interpreter by profession, and evidently a gifted one. For she was chosen to accompany President Mitterand on an official visit to his counterpart in Damascus. On the television and in newspaper pictures, Salma could be seen between the two presidents as they conferred. So those of us in this building, at least on this landing of the stair, have preened a bit at being represented in the high councils of state.

Georges could stay for just the one cup of tea. Then, being briefly both father and mother, he had to go pick up their daughter at her school. We spoke of making some plan together when Salma comes back from Damascus. It is possible we can manage it. But everything is provisional now.

I feel that even in the apartment itself. We came as trespassers into someone else's home. Then it came to be *our* home, so completely that only by a deliberate exercise of memory could we imagine any other. Now the process has begun to reverse. Again I am afflicted by the sensation of sleeping in another man's bed, sitting in his chair, eating at his table. On the walls are pictures chosen to suit another's taste. And though I have grown used to them, even find pleasure in them, they hang there for his eye, not mine.

When the concierge slips the morning mail under the door, I wonder sometimes if the envelopes will have my name on them or the next man's. When, coming back from somewhere, I put my key in the lock, I wonder sometimes if it will really turn.

That's what I mean about hating conclusions—things ending before their time has quite run out. It is some days yet, weeks actually, before we have to go anywhere. But the time remaining is shadowed and changed by this sense of termination. I begin to picture more clearly, now, that other place we live. My eyes go more often to the suitcases that, for months, lay invisible on a high storage shelf. We'll pack our lives in those and carry them away, and these rooms will remember nothing of our having stopped a while here.

If there happens to come another fine, unseasonable day, maybe there will yet be time to carry our basket across the river and up to the Parc de Saint-Cloud, to spread one more picnic on the forbidden grass. But not even that is certain. Already I am packing in my mind.

71

THE TREES BORDERING the avenue have been hung with strands of white bulbs for the season, so that when the switch is thrown just at dark the Champs-Élysées itself becomes a gigantic Christmas tree, with the floodlit arch the ornament at its top.

And it is cold now, especially when the night happens to be star-dusted and clear; not autumnally chilly, as it was only a few days ago, but serious December-cold. People wrap themselves in woolen scarves, and their breath rises in quick frosty plumes as they walk. A friend of ours who lives in Africa but who loves Paris more than any other place wrote that, when winter really came, we had to go to *Angelina* not far from the English bookstore on the Rue de Rivoli and have the hot chocolate. It is time to take his advice.

The other evening, as we waited in a line outside a theater, a woman appeared in an old fur coat and began to do a

Corner park, winter

dance—some kind of folk dance, I think it was—in the lighted area under the theater marquee. She was a woman past 60, worn-looking, and must have needed money. Her booted feet slapped and scraped the sidewalk. For accompaniment she had only her own song, sung in a voice made reedy with desperation. The people in the line, unmoved by the spirit of giving, watched her stoically, then passed on inside.

Whatever else may be said of us as tenants, our landlord's house plants, withered with neglect when we arrived in summer, have thriven under our hand. One we killed with too much watering, but the others have prospered. The *ficus* Benjamin has been our most brilliant success.

Desiccated and all but leafless at the start, it is fat with foliage again. Last week, on impulse at a store, I bought several small ornaments and a package of tinsel to hang on the fig tree. The next day a box arrived by trans-Atlantic mail from friends. Inside, with some bright packages, were other, finer ornaments and a string of miniature lights. So those have been added. The effect is definitely peculiar. Our tree will take no prize for classicism or purity of line. Its small branches droop under the glittering load, but it does not seem to object to this novel role. For, between all the hanging stuff, waxy new leaves continue happily to unfold. And by using the voltage transformer from our small appliances, we are able, for ceremonial periods each evening, to operate the lights.

So we are arrayed and ready. Outside, though, in the wider city, the holiday approaches unevenly.

Yesterday, on some errand, I had to board a métro at a busy hour, and instead of the expected crush of standing riders I was surprised to find the rear of the coach entirely empty. I went back there and started to take a seat. But before I could quite settle myself, I was overpowered by a cloying yellow stench of the most unimaginable foulness.

Hunkered in that corner of the car was a *clocharde,* a female derelict, swathed in rag garments, her face a red fleshy mass from which peered slitted, piggish eyes, dim and uncomprehending. Hardly human, the heap seemed to be. Yet it was occupied at something, filthy fingers drawing bits of unknown matter from the recesses of a plastic bag and bringing the pieces to mouth. That creature was the origin of the stink, whose dizzying authority extended for yards in every direction and whose awfulness words will not describe. From time to time the derelict clawed at matted hair, or reached a hand inside its garments to attend some itch of hidden flesh.

At other stops, other riders came on board and, spying the vacant seats, rushed to the rear of the car, only to recoil glassy-eyed with astonishment, as I had done, and join the standers at the front. Oblivious, the *clocharde* rode on and on, eating, scratching, aware only—if, indeed, aware of anything— that here, for a time, she was safe from cold.

Then my station came and I exited with relief. I had started along the foot-tunnel to my connecting train when, suddenly, there came to ear a sound so lovely that, for an instant, it stopped me in mid-step. Resonating along the network of tunnels, the music was of a beauty as overwhelming, in a different way, as the horror I had just seen. For a moment I stood and listened. Then, following the bends of the passage, I came finally to its source, a young man with eyes pressed closed beatifically as he played on a French horn the slow, pure notes of the Ave Maria.

And as the people rushed past him in the corridor on their way to somewhere, their faces changed.

72

Sᴍᴏᴋᴇ sᴘᴜʀᴛs from every chimney pot. Apartment dogs taken out on leashes tremble piteously inside their buckle-on overcoats. The Paris street people—"life's vanquished," as one newspaper writer called them—have abandoned their cardboard nests atop sidewalk grates for the shelter of underground train stations the city is keeping open all through the nights.

Even the pigeons are reported to have fled Paris in search of some warmer place.

The French, unused to real winter, have been paralyzed by a spell of weather a Midwestern American might count unexceptional for the season, but which to them is a torment of preternatural cold. The arctic air mass that has sagged down over most of Europe gives no sign of retreating for another week at the soonest. Newspapers show pictures of snow in Venice, in St. Peter's Square and on the palm trees of the Riviera. At the last count, nearly 300 people in Western Europe were known to have perished in the cold, many of those in France.

Some localities in England have been smitten by temperatures nearly as low as Moscow's. One village in Italy recorded a brutal minus 36 degrees on the Fahrenheit scale, an all-time national record. In the Jura mountains of eastern France, near the Swiss border, the mercury has fallen to the lowest readings in 100 years. Compared to those places, Paris, whose coldest overnight temperature so far has been 7 degrees above zero, is almost balmy. But it is weather for which Parisians, especially the estimated 15,000 to 20,000 vagrant and homeless poor, are unprepared.

Snow is a rarity here, and usually disappears by noon. But with cold like this the snow stays. Last night there was a fresh dusting of it and today, again, the sky is slaty gray. Chill seeps through single-pane windows and into the stones and poorly insulated walls of the old buildings. In the deep of winter on the American plain, a rise to 7 degrees sometimes is seen as a warming trend—a temperature at which folks venture out again to start their frozen cars. But here it is a catastrophe through which people stumble numb and disbelieving.

Most of them do, anyway. Not all. In the shop on the corner of our street, a man this morning asked the butcher, Monsieur Leclerc, if it was cold enough to suit him. Ruddy-faced, already warmed by the day's first several glasses of Pernod, Monsieur Leclerc replied with cheerful understatement.

"In such weather," he said, "you find no flies."

73

THE YOUNG MAN stepped into the elevator behind me, eliciting the small protocol that is necessary in our building when two strangers ride up together.

"What floor?" I asked him. *"Sixième,"* he said—the sixth. I pushed the button for five.

The elevator is an antique machine, whose control panel has no memory. You push one button and proceed to that floor. Then another button must be pushed for the next stop. Unless this is done in ascending order, the last passenger can wind up making an extensive tour of the shaft. So I pushed my button first.

"You live on six," I said. We rode past two and three. "Would you happen to know the piano player?"

He nodded, surprised. We passed four.

"I *am* the piano player."

The elevator shuddered to a stop, and seizing his arm I

dragged him out into the gloom of the landing. He looked distinctly uneasy. "You can't be the piano player," I told him. "We've already decided you're a middle-aged woman." Although tall, he was, as I've said, only a young man. And in the face of such sudden craziness, his unease was turning to genuine alarm.

"I promise you," he whined. "I am the piano player."

"Of the sixth floor?"

"Yes, of the *sixième étage*."

Keeping hold of his arm with one hand, I unlocked our door with the other and pulled him inside. My daughters were late coming from school, or I would have introduced him around. But my wife was there.

"This—" I announced importantly. "*This* is the Upstairs Piano Player."

He began to relax. He seemed relieved to know there was a woman in my life. But still grinning uncomfortably, he looked first at one then the other of us—then pointed at the ceiling.

"Do I disturb you?" he asked.

"We knew you weren't a student," I told him. "Because you never go to class. And if you were old, you wouldn't have the strength to play 10 hours a day. And you couldn't be a man, or you'd have a job."

"Yes . . . well."

"So we've decided you are a woman. A middle-aged woman, and very talented."

His nervousness was coming back. He was, he said, 19 years old, a student in the university. But he went only irregularly to his classes, so they did not interfere with his practice at the piano. Yes, he said, he would like someday to play concerts. But all the same, for insurance, he planned to take a degree in chemistry and physics. He explained all this while backing toward the door.

"We noticed a change a couple of months ago," I told him.

"Your music got sweeter, more sentimental."

"Yes . . . well," he said, opening the door behind him and retreating hastily toward the elevator.

"We've decided you are in love with a Perrier salesman from Lyon."

That was several days ago. His piano bench just scraped on the floor above us. After a brief rest for supper, he has resumed playing. His music seems to have turned sad again, for reasons I can't explain. But at least one mystery that bedeviled us now is solved.

The other mystery, mentioned at the very beginning of our time here, was the happy and yet somehow secret smile of Madame Freguin, our concierge—a smile which, I noted then, could be seen to intensify both in happiness and secrecy when her husband, Jean-Pierre, was anywhere nearby.

I encountered her one recent morning in the lobby, when she had just come from delivering the mail to more than 60 doors and sweeping the carpets on all 10 landings of the building. It was still two hours until noon, and she looked already tired.

"Jamais fini!" she said—it's never finished.

But then, in her unfailing good nature, she could not help smiling, a smile of happiness with no longer a hint of mystery in it. Madame Freguin has given up trying to seem just plump and has put on a maternity dress. She and Jean-Pierre have no more secret to keep.

74

As I write this, a winter morning fog comes eddying along the street, wrapping the corners of the buildings, obscuring distances. Paris can be lovely in such a mood. Steam beads the windows of the brasseries where men stand to take their early coffee. The dark figures of people who pass by huddled in their coats are seen against a backdrop that seems more than ever aged and ageless.

Time shortens.

Last week my wife half-awoke in the night, imagining a cat had stirred beside her in the bed. The animals are something we have missed—so keenly that, when she told me about that afterward, I envied her even the illusion of a cat.

AFTERWORD . . .

The years would accumulate in a rush. Almost before they knew it, all their lives would change. Two would go away to have their own careers, their own families, to make their own adventures. And two would stay behind, grown sedentary and perfectly happy with staying—filled up with memories.

But always when they would come together at Christmas one particular memory would be clear as yesterday, of a season in the past, far from friends and customary places. A time when, more than any before or ever again after, they were just four together.

"Do you remember our funny tree?" one of them would ask. A potted fig tree, it had been, not an evergreen.

"With not very much under it."

"Do you remember when we went off to Italy skiing and there wasn't any snow? Well, hardly any."

"And how the train at Chambéry started off with the two of us still on it? And you ran after it along the platform and made the engineer stop to let us off. We were *so-ooooh* scared."

"That's the only time I ever stopped a train."

"Then, at the border, we had to change again to the little Italian train. And in the four coaches there were only two other people besides us."

"Do you remember," one of them would ask, "after we went through the tunnel into Italy, the smell of the train station in the little town?"

"Of horses and straw. Like a stable. Like some very old mountain village in the night."

"Frosty cold. And high up in whatever valley that was."

"And no snow."

"Hardly any at all."

210

"But you two skied every day."

"And you two stayed down in the town some days. And went to the market. And were warm all day at the hotel."

"Not warm. The hotel didn't have much heat."

"Then the week was up, and we came home. And you were careful not to leave us on any trains."

"One train's enough to run after."

"And we turned on the lights of the tree, and sang to it the way we always used to: *Oh Christmas fig, oh Christmas fig, how beautiful are your branches . . .*"

"There were lights in the trees along our street. And Christmas carols were playing in the store."

"And in the morning we got warm croissants at La Fromentine. And then opened the packages —"

"There weren't many."

"We opened the ones there were, though. And it was as good as any Christmas ever."

"It's been a long time."

"But it seems like just last year."

"So look at us, will you. You two grown up to be women. And us gotten old."

"Not old!"

"Well, certainly older."

"A funny thing," one of them would say. "I don't remember once wishing we were somewhere else."

"Or me. Home was always the easiest place to be, because you know where home was, then?"

"Paris?"

"Anywhere we were four together."

But all that would be a long, long time from now. With years between to use, and other memories still to make.